The Threat Intelligence Handbook

Second Edition

Moving Toward a Security Intelligence Program

Edited by Zane Pokorny
Foreword by Christopher Ahlberg, Ph.D.

CYBEREDGE
PRESS

The Threat Intelligence Handbook, Second Edition

Published by:
CyberEdge Group, LLC
1997 Annapolis Exchange Parkway
Suite 300
Annapolis, MD 21401
(800) 327-8711
www.cyber-edge.com

For general information on CyberEdge Group research and marketing consulting services, or to create a custom *Definitive Guide* book for your organization, contact our sales department at 800-327-8711 or info@cyber-edge.com.

ISBN: 978-1-948939-06-5 (paperback)
ISBN: 978-1-948939-07-2 (eBook)

Printed in the United States of America.

10 9 8 7 6 5 4 3 2 1

Publisher's Acknowledgements

CyberEdge Group thanks the following individuals for their respective contributions:

Copy Editor: Susan Shuttleworth
Graphic Design: Debbi Stocco
Production Coordinator: Jon Friedman

Contributors

Zane Pokorny (editor and contributor) is a technical writer for Recorded Future's research team, Insikt Group. He has a background in research and report writing for nongovernmental organizations.

Andrei Barysevich (contributor) specializes in the analysis of intelligence from cybercriminal communities at Recorded Future. Andrei has worked as an independent e-commerce fraud researcher, and a private consultant for the FBI's cybercrime unit.

Levi Gundert (contributor) has spent the past 20 years in both the government and the private sector, defending networks, arresting international criminals, and uncovering nation-state adversaries. He has held senior information security leadership positions across technology and financial services startups and enterprises. He is a trusted risk advisor to Fortune 500 companies, and a prolific speaker, blogger, and columnist.

Allan Liska (contributor) is a senior security architect at Recorded Future. Allan has more than 15 years of experience in information security, authoring numerous books and working as both a security practitioner and an ethical hacker.

Maggie McDaniel (contributor) is senior director of Recorded Future's Insikt Group research team. With more than 15 years of experience in threat intelligence tradecraft, analysis, and production, Maggie's previous roles include director of intelligence production at Fidelity Investments.

John Wetzel (contributor) heads up training at Recorded Future. John's previous role was as a counterintelligence special agent with the Department of Defense, where he worked with the U.S. defense community to defend against foreign threats targeting the nation's technologies.

Foreword by **Dr. Christopher Ahlberg**, co-founder and CEO, Recorded Future.

Table of Contents

Foreword to the Second Edition

When I started Recorded Future about a decade ago, I made a bet. I wagered that the future of information security lay with moving from a reactive to a proactive approach, where security professionals would use threat intelligence gathered from every corner of the internet to give us insight into the intentions and techniques of our adversaries.

In the 10 years since, a lot has changed in the world of cybersecurity. It seems every day's news is filled with stories about major data breaches affecting millions of people, whole municipalities having their networks held hostage by ransomware attacks, and nation-state actors manipulating elections, influencing public opinion, and persecuting their enemies. "Cyber warfare" is becoming a familiar term — today we can't imagine warfare without a cyber element playing a crucial role at every level of operations.

Our most precious information is no longer kept in locked file cabinets or safes, but on our computers and in the cloud. It's just not enough to lock down your endpoints and keep alert for suspicious behavior inside your own network. The threat landscape is way too big for that now. We need to get real-time, automated threat intelligence in front of the people who can take action quickly, helping them stop threats fast — sometimes before they even happen.

That goal motivates all the work we do at Recorded Future. Our work is based on three principles:

1. Threat intelligence must provide the context to make informed decisions and take action.

Threat intelligence needs to be timely, clear, and actionable. It has to come at the right time, in a form that is understandable. It should enrich your knowledge, not complicate the decision-making process. It should help put everybody in your organization on the same page.

2. People and machines work better together.

Machines can process and categorize raw data orders exponentially faster than humans. On the other hand, humans can perform intuitive, big-picture analysis much better than any artificial intelligence — as long as they're not overwhelmed with sorting through huge data sets and doing tedious research. When people and machines are paired, each works smarter, saving time and money, reducing human burnout, and improving security overall.

3. Threat intelligence is for everyone.

No matter what security role you play, threat intelligence makes a difference. It's not a separate domain of security — it's context that helps you work smarter, whether you're staffing a SOC, managing vulnerabilities, or making high-level security decisions. But to make things easier, not harder, threat intelligence should integrate with the solutions and workflows you already rely on and should be easy to implement.

At Recorded Future, we believe wholeheartedly in these core principles, and our approach has been validated in the year since the first edition of this handbook came out. We're helping stop threats in the security departments of 90 of Fortune's top 100 companies in the United States, not to mention countless organizations and government institutions around the world. And we've grown to over 400 employees now from 40 countries.

We continue to innovate and improve our intelligence solutions. That includes this handbook, which has been updated with three new chapters for its second edition. We've given this edition a subtitle of "Moving Toward a Security Intelligence Program," and these new chapters address this shift that every organization is going to have to take: toward security intelligence, a new paradigm of security of which threat intelligence is only one part.

Threats are coming from everywhere (open web, dark web, partners, internal, brand attacks) and a true view of your entire threat surface is needed or else you are vulnerable. That takes a security solution that encompasses threat intelligence that you can correlate with internal network data, digital risk protection, and third-party risk management.

We hope this handbook can play its part in helping you make this shift by offering practical information and advice that you can apply today to solve real-world problems with threat intelligence.

I want to thank everyone who has contributed to the contents of this handbook: our users and customers, industry experts, and the Recorded Future staff listed on the **Contributors** page at the beginning of this volume.

We hope you will find this updated book an informative companion as you apply threat intelligence to address the security challenges you face.

Christopher Ahlberg, Ph.D.
Co-Founder and CEO
Recorded Future

Introduction

Moving Toward a Security Intelligence Program

Today, cyber threats are coming from everywhere — the open web and dark web, but also partners and other third parties, brand attacks, and internal threats — and digital business risk is at an all-time high. This leaves everyone without a true, comprehensive view of their entire threat landscape vulnerable.

A comprehensive cybersecurity strategy requires the implementation of techniques and technology to proactively reduce risk and stop threats fast. This book explains how security intelligence helps teams working in security operations, incident response, vulnerability management, risk analysis, threat analysis, fraud prevention, and security leadership make better, faster decisions and amplify their impact.

We call this approach "security intelligence" because it goes beyond just threat intelligence (though threat intelligence remains a central pillar) and also encompasses digital risk protection and third-party risk management. It's a framework that amplifies the effectiveness of security teams and tools by exposing unknown threats, informing better decisions, and driving a common understanding to ultimately accelerate risk reduction across the organization.

In this second edition of the Handbook, you'll find a completely new introductory chapter on threat intelligence that breaks down what threat intelligence is and how every security function benefits from it, as well as two entirely new chapters — one on third-party risk reduction, and one on digital risk protection. Together, these three pillars of security intelligence provide the comprehensive view of both your internal and external threat landscape that every organization needs today to reduce cyber risk and stay ahead of threats of all kinds.

This is only the start. Recorded Future will soon be publishing new materials that go into more depth on these three areas of security intelligence, how they reinforce each other, and how they can be addressed by a single technology platform. For more information, check regularly at recordedfuture.com.

— The Recorded Future Team

Chapters at a Glance

Section 1: What Is Threat Intelligence?

Chapter 1, "What Is Threat Intelligence," outlines the value of threat intelligence and the roles of operational and strategic threat intelligence.

Chapter 2, "The Threat Intelligence Lifecycle," describes the phases of the threat intelligence lifecycle and looks at sources of threat intelligence.

Section 2: Applications of Threat Intelligence

Chapter 3, "Threat Intelligence for Security Operations," explores how intelligence provides context for triage and helps the SOC team make better decisions.

Chapter 4, "Threat Intelligence for Incident Response," discusses how intelligence can minimize reactivity in incident response and presents three use cases.

Chapter 5, "Threat Intelligence for Vulnerability Management," examines how intelligence helps prioritize vulnerabilities based on true risk to the enterprise.

Chapter 6, "Threat Intelligence for Security Leaders," explores how building a comprehensive threat intelligence capability can help CISOs manage risk and make effective investment decisions.

Chapter 7, "Threat Intelligence for Risk Analysis," explains the value of risk models and how intelligence can provide hard data about attack probabilities and costs.

Chapter 8, "Threat Intelligence for Fraud Prevention," enumerates how intelligence can help anticipate and defeat fraud.

Chapter 9, "Threat Intelligence for Reducing Third-Party Risk," suggests how intelligence can help assess supply chain partners and reduce third party risk.

Chapter 10, "Threat Intelligence for Digital Risk Protection," illustrates how intelligence can help identify and remediate brand impersonation and data breaches.

Section 3: Your Threat Intelligence Program

Chapter 11, "Analytical Frameworks for Threat Intelligence," explains how three leading threat frameworks provide useful structures for thinking about attacks.

Chapter 12, "Your Threat Intelligence Journey," provides suggestions on how to start simple and scale up a threat intelligence program.

Chapter 13, "Developing the Core Threat Intelligence Team," describes how a dedicated team can take threat intelligence to a new level.

Helpful Icons

TIP

Tips provide practical advice that you can apply in your own organization.

DON'T FORGET

When you see this icon, take note, as the related content contains key information that you won't want to forget.

CAUTION

Proceed with caution because if you don't, it may prove costly to you and your organization.

TECH TALK

Content associated with this icon is more technical in nature and is intended for IT practitioners.

ON THE WEB

Want to learn more? Follow the corresponding URL to discover additional content available on the web.

Section 1: What Is Threat Intelligence?

Chapter 1

What Is Threat Intelligence?

In this chapter

- Understand why threat intelligence is important
- Learn about operational and strategic threat intelligence
- Explore the role of threat feeds and the value of monitoring private channels

"Every battle is won before it is ever fought."

— Sun Tzu

What Have You Heard About Threat Intelligence?

You may have heard threat intelligence discussed at a conference or trade show. Perhaps you were informed by a consultant that threat intelligence provides external context for security decisions. Maybe you read a report about state-sponsored attacks and want to know how to protect your enterprise. You have probably noticed that in organizations from multinational enterprises to midmarket companies, information security teams are racing to add threat intelligence to their security programs.

But you may also have heard some misconceptions: that threat intelligence is just data feeds and PDF reports, is simply a research service for the incident response team, or requires a dedicated team of high-priced, elite analysts.

These are fallacies! In this book, we will show that threat intelligence:

- ☑ Includes information and analysis from a rich array of sources, presented in ways that make it easy to understand and use
- ☑ Is immensely valuable to all the major teams in the cybersecurity organization
- ☑ Can help every security function save time
- ☑ Can be handled mostly by existing security staff (with the right tools and support)

Why Is Threat Intelligence Important?

Today, the cybersecurity industry faces numerous challenges — increasingly persistent and devious threat actors; a daily flood of data full of extraneous information and false alarms across multiple, unconnected security systems; and a serious shortage of skilled professionals.

And although around $124 billion will be spent worldwide on cybersecurity products and services in 2019, throwing money at these problems won't be enough. Right now:

- ☑ Three-quarters of security organizations are experiencing skills shortages
- ☑ 44 percent of security alerts go uninvestigated
- ☑ 66 percent of companies are breached at least once

Sources: Gartner Forecast Analysis: Information Security, Worldwide, 2Q18 Update; ESG & ISSA Research Report: The Life and Times of Cybersecurity Professionals 2018; Cisco 2017 Annual Cybersecurity Report; Ponemon 2019 Cost of Data Breach Study

Digital technologies lie at the heart of nearly every industry today. The automation and greater connectedness they afford are revolutionizing the world, but they're also bringing increased vulnerability to cyberattacks.

Threat intelligence is knowledge that allows you to prevent and mitigate attacks on digital systems. Rooted in data, threat intelligence provides context like who's attacking you, what their motivation and capabilities are, and what indicators of compromise (IOCs) in your systems to look for. It helps you make informed decisions about your security.

Who Can Benefit From Threat Intelligence?

Everyone! Threat intelligence is widely imagined to be the domain of elite analysts. In reality, it adds value across security functions for organizations of all sizes. For example:

☑ **Security operations teams** are routinely unable to process the overwhelming flow of alerts they receive. Threat intelligence can be integrated with the security solutions they already use, helping them automatically prioritize and filter alerts and other threats.

☑ **Vulnerability management teams** need to accurately prioritize the most important vulnerabilities. Threat intelligence provides access to external insights and context that helps them differentiate immediate threats to their specific enterprise from merely potential threats.

☑ **Fraud prevention**, **risk analysis**, and other **high-level security staff** are challenged to understand the current threat landscape. Threat intelligence provides key insights on threat actors, their intentions and targets, and their tactics, techniques, and procedures (TTPs).

Figure 1-1 lists metrics that show the dramatic improvements in security and efficiency that a threat intelligence program can provide.

Topline Metrics

Overall more efficient IT security teams	3-year ROI	To payback
32%	**284%**	**4 Months**

Security Operational Efficiencies

Less staff time spent compiling security reports	Earlier identification of threats	Faster resolution of security threats
34%	**10x**	**63%**

Risk Reduction

22%	**86%**	**$1M**
More security threats identified before impact	Reduction in unplanned downtime	Potential penalties/fines per breach avoided

Figure 1-1: A threat intelligence program can produce dramatic improvements in security and operational efficiency. Source of data: IDC

Section 2 of this book is devoted to exploring these and other security use cases in greater detail.

Data and Information Are Not Intelligence

Before we go any further, let's clear up any confusion about data, information, and intelligence.

These three terms are sometimes used without much care. For example, some threat feeds are advertised as intelligence when they are actually just packages of data. Frequently, organizations incorporate threat data feeds into their network only to find that they can't process all the extra data, which only adds to the burden on analysts trying to triage threats. In contrast, threat intelligence lightens that burden by helping the analysts decide what to prioritize and what to ignore. The table in Figure 1-2 highlights important distinctions.

> **Data** consists of discrete facts and statistics gathered as the basis for further analysis.

> **Information** is multiple data points combined to answer specific questions.

> **Intelligence** analyzes data and information to uncover patterns and stories that inform decision-making.

Figure 1-2: Distinctions between data, information, and intelligence

In cybersecurity:

- ☑ Data is usually just indicators such as IP addresses, URLs, or hashes. Data doesn't tell us much without analysis.

- ☑ Information answers questions like, "How many times has my organization been mentioned on social media this month?" Although this is a far more useful output than the raw data, it still doesn't directly inform a specific action.

- ☑ Intelligence is the product of a cycle of identifying questions and goals, collecting relevant data, processing and analyzing that data, producing actionable intelligence, and distributing that intelligence. We'll look at the threat intelligence lifecycle in greater depth in Chapter 2.

The relationship between data, information, and intelligence is illustrated in Figure 1-3.

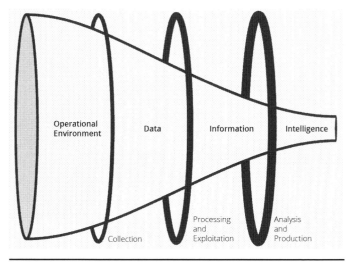

Figure 1-3: The relationship between data, information, and intelligence

Two Types of Threat Intelligence

Threat intelligence is a broad concept, one that is really made up of two kinds of intelligence — **operational** and **strategic**. These two types of intelligence vary in their sources, the audiences they serve, and the formats they appear in.

The purpose in making this distinction is in recognizing that the various security functions have different goals and degrees of technical knowledge. Like we said above, intelligence needs to be actionable — but because the responsibilities of a vulnerability management team differ significantly from those of a CISO, "actionability" has distinct implications for each, and the form and content of the intelligence they'll benefit the most from will vary.

Operational Threat Intelligence

Operational threat intelligence is knowledge about ongoing cyberattacks, events, and campaigns. It gives incident response teams specialized insights that help them understand the nature, intent, and timing of specific attacks as they are occurring. It's generally sourced from machines.

Operational intelligence is sometimes referred to as **technical threat intelligence**, because it usually includes technical information about attacks, such as which attack vectors are being used, what vulnerabilities are being exploited, and what command and control domains are being employed by attackers. This kind of intelligence is often most useful to personnel directly involved in the defense of an organization, such as system architects, administrators, and security staff.

A common source of technical information is threat data feeds. These usually focus on a single type of threat indicator, such as malware hashes or suspicious domains. As we discuss below, threat data feeds supply input for threat intelligence, but by themselves are not threat intelligence.

One use of operational threat intelligence is to guide improvements to existing security controls and processes and speed up incident response. Because operational intelligence can answer urgent questions unique to your organization — such as, "Is this critical vulnerability, which is being exploited in my industry, present in my systems?" — a solution that integrates with data from your network is crucial.

Strategic Threat Intelligence

Strategic threat intelligence provides a wide overview of an organization's threat landscape. It's most helpful for informing high-level decisions by executives, and the content is generally business oriented and is presented through reports or briefings — materials that really can't be generated by machines, but only by humans with expertise.

This kind of intelligence requires the human element because it takes time and thought to evaluate and test new adversary tactics, techniques, and procedures against existing security controls. Pieces of this process can be automated, but a human brain is largely required to complete the exercise.

Good strategic intelligence should provide insight into the risks associated with certain actions, broad patterns in threat actor tactics and targets, geopolitical events and trends, and similar topics.

Common sources of information for strategic threat intelligence include:

- ☑ Policy documents from nation-states or nongovernmental organizations
- ☑ News from local and national media, articles in industry- and subject-specific publications, and input from subject-matter experts
- ☑ White papers, research reports, and other content produced by security organizations

Organizations must set strategic threat intelligence requirements by asking focused, specific questions. Analysts with expertise outside of typical cybersecurity skills — in particular, a strong understanding of sociopolitical and business concepts — are needed to gather and interpret strategic threat intelligence.

DON'T FORGET

Some parts of the production of strategic threat intelligence should be automated. Although the final product is non-technical, producing effective strategic threat intelligence takes deep research and massive volumes of data, often across multiple languages. These challenges can make initial data collection and processing too difficult to perform manually, even for those rare analysts who possess the right language skills, technical background, and tradecraft. A threat intelligence solution that automates data collection and processing helps reduce this burden and allows analysts with less expertise to work more effectively.

The Role of Threat Data Feeds

We mentioned earlier that data is not intelligence, and that threat data feeds can overwhelm analysts already burdened with countless daily alerts and notifications. But when used correctly, threat data feeds can provide valuable raw material for threat intelligence.

Threat data feeds are real-time streams of data that provide information on potential cyber threats and risks. They're usually lists of simple indicators or artifacts focused on a single area of interest, like suspicious domains, hashes, bad IPs, or malicious code. They can provide an easy way to get quick, real-time looks at the threat landscape.

But many feeds, especially the free ones, are filled with errors, redundancies, and false positives. That's why it's important to select high-quality data feeds.

Evaluating Threat Data Feeds

Use these criteria to assess threat data feeds for your organization:

Data sources: Cyber threat intelligence feeds pull their data from all kinds of sources, many of which are not relevant for your organization. For example, you will get the most value from data gathered from organizations in your industry.

Transparency of sources: Knowing where the data is coming from will help you evaluate its relevance and usefulness.

Percentage of unique data: Some paid feeds are just collections of data coming from other feeds, so they list the same items several times.

Periodicity of data: How long is the data relevant? Is it related to specific, immediate activity, and does it provide strategic intelligence on long-term trends?

Measurable outcomes: Calculating the measurable outcomes of a particular feed usually involves tracking the correlation rate, which is the percentage of alerts that correspond with your internal telemetry in a given week, month, or quarter.

Instead of viewing dozens of feeds separately, use a threat intelligence platform that combines them all into a single feed, removes duplicates and false positives, compares them with internal telemetry, and generates prioritized alerts. The most powerful threat intelligence platforms even allow organizations to create custom threat intelligence feeds, or curate and set up automated alerting.

The Role of Private Channels and the Dark Web

Threat data feeds and publicly available information are not the only external sources of data for threat intelligence. Vital operational and strategic intelligence on specific attacks, attacker TTPs, political goals of hacktivists and state actors, and other key topics can be gathered by infiltrating or breaking into private channels of communication used by threat groups. These include encrypted messaging apps and exclusive forums on the dark web.

However, there are barriers to gathering this kind of intelligence:

- ☑ **Access**: Threat groups may communicate over private and encrypted channels, or require some proof of identification.

- ☑ **Language:** Activity on many forums is carried out in languages like Russian, Chinese, Indonesian, or Arabic, using local slang and specialized jargon.

- ☑ **Noise:** It can be difficult or impossible to manually gather good intelligence from high-volume sources like chat rooms and social media.

- ☑ **Obfuscation**: To avoid detection, many threat groups employ obfuscation tactics like using codenames.

Overcoming these barriers requires a large investment in tools and expertise for monitoring private channels — or the use of threat intelligence service providers that have already made that investment.

TIP Look for threat intelligence solutions and services that employ machine learning processes for automated data collection on a large scale. A solution that uses natural language processing, for example, can gather information from foreign-language sources without needing human expertise to decipher it.

Chapter 2

The Threat Intelligence Lifecycle

- Examine the phases of the threat intelligence lifecycle
- Review sources of threat intelligence
- Look at the roles of threat intelligence tools and human analysts

"You have to believe in your process."

— Tom Brady

The Six Phases of the Threat Intelligence Lifecycle

Threat intelligence is built on analytic techniques honed over several decades by government and military agencies. Traditional intelligence focuses on six distinct phases that make up what is called the "intelligence cycle":Threat intelligence provides an antidote to many of these problems. Among other uses, it can be employed to filter out false alarms, speed up triage, and simplify incident analysis.

1. Direction
2. Collection
3. Processing
4. Analysis
5. Dissemination
6. Feedback

Figure 2-1 shows how those six phases align with threat intelligence.

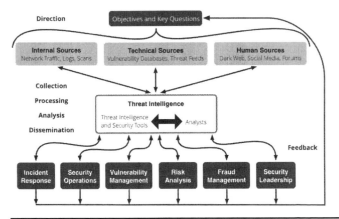

Figure 2-1: Threat intelligence and the six phases of the intelligence cycle.

Direction

The direction phase of the lifecycle is when you set goals for the threat intelligence program. This involves understanding and articulating:

☑ The information assets and business processes that need to be protected

☑ The potential impacts of losing those assets or interrupting those processes

☑ The types of threat intelligence that the security organization requires to protect assets and respond to threats

☑ Priorities about what to protect

Once high-level intelligence needs are determined, an organization can formulate questions that channel the need for information into discrete requirements. For example, if a goal is to understand likely adversaries, one logical question would be, "Which actors on underground forums are actively soliciting data concerning our organization?"

A Library of Goals

Recorded Future has created a list of pre-configured intelligence goals that includes the most common intelligence requirements of Global 500 organizations. This list helps companies starting out with threat intelligence think about their issues and priorities and decide how threat intelligence can be plugged into their existing processes. Selected goals from this library are included in the appendix of this book.

Adversarial models such as the Lockheed-Martin Cyber Kill Chain and the MITRE Adversarial Tactics, Techniques & Common Knowledge (ATT&CK) matrix (discussed in Chapter 11), can also help companies focus on the types of threat intelligence they need to collect to prevent breaches.

Collection

Collection is the process of gathering information to address the most important intelligence requirements. Information gathering can occur organically through a variety of means, including:

- ☑ Pulling metadata and logs from internal networks and security devices
- ☑ Subscribing to threat data feeds from industry organizations and cybersecurity vendors
- ☑ Holding conversations and targeted interviews with knowledgeable sources
- ☑ Scanning open source news and blogs
- ☑ Scraping and harvesting websites and forums
- ☑ Infiltrating closed sources such as dark web forums

The data collected typically will be a combination of finished information, such as intelligence reports from cybersecurity experts and vendors, and raw data, like malware signatures or leaked credentials on a paste site.

Threat Intelligence Sources

Technical sources (e.g., threat feeds) — Available in huge quantities, often for free. Technical sources are easy to integrate with existing security technologies but often contain a high proportion of false positives and outdated results.

Media (e.g., security websites, vendor research) — These sources often provide useful information about emerging threats but are hard to connect with technical indicators in order to measure risk.

Social media — Social channels offer huge amounts of valuable data, but it comes at a price. False positives and misinformation are rampant, so determining which insights are usable requires a tremendous amount of cross-referencing with other sources.

Threat actor forums — Specifically designed to host relevant discussions, forums offer some of the most helpful insights available anywhere. Once again, though, analysis and cross-referencing are essential to determine what is truly valuable.

The dark web (including markets and forums) — While often the birthplace of hugely valuable intelligence, dark web sources can be extremely hard to access, particularly those that play host to serious criminal communities.

DON'T FORGET You need multiple sources of intelligence to get a complete picture of potential and actual threats. As shown in Figure 2-1, they include **internal sources** like firewall and router logs, network packet capture tools, and vulnerability scans, **technical sources** such as vulnerability databases and threat data feeds, and **human sources**, including traditional and social media, cybersecurity forums and blogs, and dark web forums. Missing any one of these can slow down investigations and cause gaps in remediation.

TIP Automate! Analysts should spend as little time as possible collecting data, and as much time as possible evaluating and communicating threat information.

ON THE WEB Confused about the difference between threat intelligence sources, feeds, platforms, and providers? Read the Recorded Future blog post "Threat Intelligence: Difference Between Platforms and Providers."

Processing

Processing is the transformation of collected information into a format usable by the organization. Almost all raw data collected needs to be processed in some manner, whether by humans or machines.

Different collection methods often require different means of processing. Human reports may need to be correlated and ranked, deconflicted, and checked. An example might be extracting IP addresses from a security vendor's report and adding them to a CSV file for importing to a security information and event management (SIEM) product. In a more technical area, processing might involve extracting indicators from an email, enriching them with other information, and then communicating with endpoint protection tools for automated blocking.

TIP Automate more! With the right tools, most processing workflows, as well as most collection processes, can be automated. For example, a security automation tool might identify a suspicious IOC, then conduct a sequence of checks to bring context to the IOC. This saves the analyst from having to conduct those checks manually.

Analysis

Analysis is a human process that turns processed information into intelligence that can inform decisions. Depending on the circumstances, the decisions might involve whether to investigate a potential threat, what actions to take immediately to block an attack, how to strengthen security controls, or how much investment in additional security resources is justified.

DON'T FORGET Analysts must have a clear understanding of who is going to be using their intelligence and what decisions those people make. You want the intelligence you deliver to be perceived as actionable, not as academic. Most of this book is devoted to giving you a clear picture of exactly how threat intelligence can improve decision making and actions in different areas of cybersecurity.

The form in which the information is presented is especially important. It is useless and wasteful to collect and process information and then deliver it in a form that can't be understood and used by the decision maker.

For example, if you want to communicate with non-technical leaders, your report must:

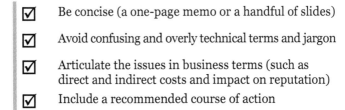

- ☑ Be concise (a one-page memo or a handful of slides)
- ☑ Avoid confusing and overly technical terms and jargon
- ☑ Articulate the issues in business terms (such as direct and indirect costs and impact on reputation)
- ☑ Include a recommended course of action

Some intelligence may need to be delivered in a variety of formats for different audiences, say, by a live video feed and a PowerPoint presentation. Not all intelligence needs to be digested via a formal report. Successful threat intelligence teams provide continual technical reporting to other security teams with external context around IOCs, malware, threat actors, vulnerabilities, and threat trends.

Dissemination

Dissemination involves getting the finished intelligence output to the places it needs to go.

As illustrated in Figure 2-1, most cybersecurity organizations have at least six teams that can benefit from threat intelligence. For each of these audiences you need to ask:

- ☑ What threat intelligence do they need, and how can external information support their activities?
- ☑ How should the intelligence be presented to make it easily understandable and actionable for that audience?
- ☑ How often should we provide updates and other information?
- ☑ Through what media should the intelligence be disseminated?
- ☑ How should we follow up if they have questions?

Feedback

As you have no doubt gathered, we believe that it is critically important to understand your overall intelligence priorities and the requirements of the security teams that will be consuming the threat intelligence. Their needs guide all phases of the intelligence lifecycle and tell you:

☑ What types of data to collect

☑ How to process and enrich the data to turn it into useful information

☑ How to analyze the information and present it as actionable intelligence

☑ To whom each type of intelligence must be disseminated, how quickly it needs to be disseminated, and how fast to respond to questions

You need regular feedback to make sure you understand the requirements of each group, and to make adjustments as their requirements and priorities change.

For every "customer" team, establish both a channel for fast, informal feedback (such as an email address, an internal forum, or a team collaboration tool) and a formal, structured surveying process (such as an online survey or a quarterly face-to-face meeting). The informal channel helps you react and adjust immediately, while the structured survey ensures that you get input from everyone and can track your progress over time.

Tools and People

Tools are essential to automating the collection, processing, and dissemination steps in the intelligence lifecycle and to supporting and accelerating analysis. Without the right tools, analysts will spend all their time on the mechanical aspects of these tasks and never have time for real analysis

Most mature threat intelligence groups leverage two types of tools:

- ☑ Threat intelligence solutions that are designed to collect, process, and analyze all types of threat data from internal, technical, and human sources
- ☑ Existing security tools, such as SIEMs and security analytics tools, which collect and correlate security events and log data

Human analysts are equally if not more important. You can't rely on tools to interview security experts and probe closed dark web forums, and you need people to analyze and synthesize intelligence for the people in the security organization and management who will consume it.

The analysts do not need to belong to a central, elite threat intelligence department. While someone needs to take an organization-wide view of the threat intelligence function, make decisions about resources and priorities, and track progress, we have seen many successful organizational structures. You could have a central group with dedicated threat intelligence analysts, or a small group inside the incident response (IR) or security operations center (SOC) organizations. Alternatively, members of the different cybersecurity groups can be responsible for analyzing threat intelligence for their colleagues.

In Chapter 12 we discuss how the organizational structure often evolves as the threat intelligence function matures. In Chapter 13 we provide advice on how to organize a core threat intelligence team.

Section 2: Applications of Threat Intelligence

Chapter 3

Threat Intelligence for Security Operations

- See how "alert fatigue" risks undoing the good work of security operations centers (SOCs)
- Understand the value of context for improving triage
- Learn how threat intelligence can lead to less wasted time and better decisions by the SOC team

"Being the worst makes you first."

— Sign in hospital emergency room

Most security operations center (SOC) teams find themselves hostages to the huge volumes of alerts generated by the networks they monitor. Triaging these alerts takes too long, and many are never investigated at all. "Alert fatigue" leads analysts to take alerts less seriously than they should.

Threat intelligence provides an antidote to many of these problems. Among other uses, it can be employed to filter out false alarms, speed up triage, and simplify incident analysis.

Responsibilities of the SOC Team

On paper, the responsibilities of the SOC team seem simple:

- ☑ **Monitor** for potential threats
- ☑ **Detect** suspicious network activity
- ☑ **Contain** active threats
- ☑ **Remediate** using available technology

When a suspicious event is detected, the SOC team investigates, then works with other security teams to reduce the impact and severity of the attack. You can think of the roles and responsibilities within a SOC as being similar to those of emergency services teams responding to 911 calls, as shown in Figure 3-1.

Stage	Role	Responsibilities
Triage	Operator (911 Center) Security Analyst (SOC)	Determine the relevance and urgency of each incoming alert. Decide if the alert is legitimate and should be escalated.
First Response	First Responder (911) Incident Responder (SOC)	Determine the scope of the incident. Identify affected and vulnerable systems. Recommend actions to contain the effects.
Investigation	Detective (911) Threat Hunter (SOC)	Determine root causes and weaknesses in defenses. Recommend actions to prevent recurrences.

Figure 3-1: The roles and responsibilities of emergency services teams and SOC teams are similar.

The Overwhelming Volume of Alerts

Over the past several years, most enterprises have added new types of threat detection technologies to their networks. Every tool sounds the alarm when it sees anomalous or suspicious behavior. In combination, these tools can create a cacophony of security alerts. Security analysts are simply unable to review, prioritize, and investigate all these alerts on their own. Because of alert fatigue, all too often they ignore alerts, chase false positives, and make mistakes.

Research confirms the magnitude of these problems. Industry analyst firm ESG asked cybersecurity professionals about their biggest security operations challenge, and 35 percent said it was "keeping up with the volume of security alerts." In its 2018 State of the SOC report, SIEM provider Exabeam revealed that SOCs are understaffed according to 45 percent of professionals who work in them, and of those, 63 percent think they could use anywhere from two to 10 additional employees. Cisco's 2018 Security Capabilities Benchmark study found that organizations can investigate only 56 percent of the security alerts they receive on a given day, and of those investigated alerts, only 34 percent are deemed legitimate (Figure 3-2).

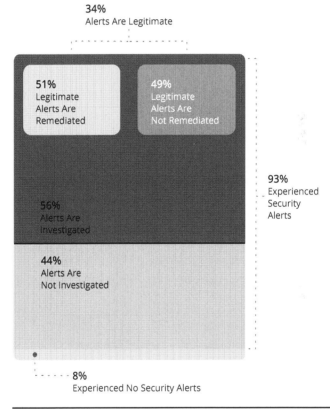

Figure 3-2: Many threat alerts are not investigated or remediated. (Source: Cisco)

Context Is King

At its heart, threat intelligence for the SOC is about enriching internal alerts with the external information and context necessary to make risk-based decisions. Context is critical for rapid triage, and also very important for scoping and containing incidents.

Triage requires lots of context

A huge part of an average SOC analyst's day is spent responding to alerts generated by internal security systems, such as SIEM or EDR technologies. Sources of internal data are vital in identifying potentially malicious network activity or a data breach.

Unfortunately, this data is often difficult to interpret in isolation. Determining if an alert is relevant and urgent requires gathering related information (context) from a wide variety of internal system logs, network devices, and security tools (Figure 3-3), *and* from external threat databases. Searching all of these threat data sources for context around each alert is hugely time consuming.

Key Aspects	Security Monitoring Requirement
Business Traffic Crossing a Boundary	Traffic exchanges are authorized and conform to security policy. Transport of malicious content and other forms of attack by manipulation of business traffic are detected and alerted.
Activity at a Boundary	Detect suspect activity indicative of the actions of an attacker attempting to breach the system boundary or other deviation from normal business behavior.
Internal Workstation, Server, or Device	Detect changes to device status and configuration from accidental or deliberate acts by a user or by malware.
Internal Network Activity	Detect suspicious activity that may indicate attacks by internal users or external attackers who have penetrated the internal network.
Network Connections	Prevent unauthorized connections to the network made by remote access, VPN, wireless, or any other transient means of network connection.
Session Activity By User and Workstation	Detect unauthorized activity and access that is suspicious or violates security policy requirements.
Alerting on Events	Be able to respond to security incidents in a time frame appropriate to the perceived criticality of the incident.
Accurate Time in Logs	Be able to correlate event data collected from disparate sources.
Data Backup Status	Be able to recover from an event that compromises the integrity or availability of information assets.

Figure 3-3: Key aspects of security monitoring and internal sources of context. (Source: UK NCSC)

Use case: Correlating and enriching alerts

An analyst attempting to triage an initial alert without access to enough context is like a person trying to understand a news story after reading just the headline. Even when the analyst has access to external information in the form of threat feeds (Figure 3-4), that information is very hard to assimilate and correlate with other data related to the alert.

2018-09-13 02:46:26	E	63.153.27.53	offline
2018-09-12 21:41:44	E	75.130.100.165	online
2018-09-12 18:54:45	E	71.172.252.50	online
2018-09-12 15:51:16	E	118.189.9.243	offline
2018-09-12 14:11:41	E	31.167.248.50	offline
2018-09-12 08:32:01	E	78.134.74.39	online
2018-09-12 05:03:02	E	42.114.73.81	offline
2018-09-12 04:56:53	E	216.59.200.206	offline
2018-09-11 11:35:10	E	183.82.97.20	offline
2018-09-11 08:59:59	E	128.2.98.139	offline
2018-09-11 08:12:12	E	47.38.231.174	offline
2018-09-11 08:01:28	E	217.36.122.251	offline
2018-09-11 07:45:59	E	107.184.160.132	offline
2018-09-11 06:45:54	E	71.75.206.192	online
2018-09-11 06:43:49	E	123.231.21.141	offline
2018-09-11 05:54:51	E	189.222.75.8	offline
2018-09-11 05:54:51	E	189.211.177.113	offline
2018-09-11 05:54:51	E	92.27.115.15	offline
2018-09-11 05:54:51	E	207.107.101.210	offline
2018-09-11 05:31:45	E	185.97.32.6	online

Figure 3-4: It is very difficult to find relevant information in a raw threat feed and correlate it with other data related to an alert.

Threat intelligence, or more precisely, information delivered through a threat intelligence solution, can completely transform the situation. Such a solution has the capability to automatically enrich threat data into intelligence and correlate it with alerts, as illustrated in Figure 3-5. The context provided might include first and most recent references to a piece of malware or a suspicious IP address, the number of sightings, associations with attack types and specific threat actors, and descriptions of the behavior of the malware or the uses of the IP address (say, as part of a botnet).

Figure 3-5: A threat intelligence solution can automatically enrich alerts with context such as previous sightings, associations with attack types and threat actors, and risk scores. (Source: Recorded Future)

This enrichment enables SOC analysts to quickly identify the most significant threats and take immediate, informed actions to resolve them.

Enrichment allows relatively junior analysts in the SOC to "punch above their weight" by making connections that otherwise would have required more experience. It also provides a form of accelerated on-the-job training by providing in-depth information about the latest threats.

TECH TALK

As an example of upskilling relatively junior analysts, suppose an alert is generated when an unknown external IP address attempts to connect over TCP port 445. Experienced analysts might know that a recent exploit for SMB has been used by ransomware to propagate itself and would identify the IP as likely compromised based on the owner, location, and open source data. Newer analysts might not be able to make these connections unaided, but contextualized threat intelligence could show them that other devices on the network use SMB on port 445 to transfer files and data between servers. It could also inform them that the new exploit and ransomware have been associated with that IP address.

Improving the "Time to No"

As important as it is for SOC analysts to gather information about real threats more quickly and accurately, there is an argument to be made that *the ability to rapidly rule out false alarms is even more important.*

Threat intelligence provides SOC staff with additional information and context needed to triage alerts promptly and with far less effort. It can prevent analysts from wasting hours pursuing alerts based on:

- ☑ Actions that are more likely to be innocuous rather than malicious
- ☑ Attacks that are not relevant to that enterprise
- ☑ Attacks for which defenses and controls are already in place

Some threat intelligence solutions automatically perform much of this filtering by customizing risk feeds to ignore or downgrade alerts that do not match organization- and industry-specific criteria.

Threat Intelligence Makes IT Security Teams 32 Percent More Efficient

A survey and analysis by IDC found that a threat intelligence solution enabled IT security teams to reduce the time needed for threat investigation, threat resolution, and security report compilation by **32 percent**, saving an average of **$640,000 annually**. In addition, the teams in the survey were able to detect **22 percent** more threats before they impacted the organization, and resolve incidents **63 percent** faster. To read the full IDC white paper, go to https://go.recordedfuture.com/idc.

Beyond Triage

As well as accelerating triage, threat intelligence can help SOC teams simplify incident analysis and containment.

For example, by revealing that a certain piece of malware is often used by cybercriminals as the first step in an attack on financial applications, the SOC team can start monitoring those applications more closely and home in on other evidence of that attack type.

Chapter 4

Threat Intelligence for Incident Response

- Learn how threat intelligence can minimize reactivity
- Review characteristics of threat intelligence solutions that make them effective for meeting incident response challenges
- Explore use cases for using threat intelligence for incident response

"Care shouldn't start in the emergency room."

— James Douglas

Of all security groups, incident response teams are perhaps the most highly stressed. Among the reasons:

☑ Cyber incident volumes have increased steadily for two decades.

☑ Threats have become more complex and harder to analyze; staying on top of the shifting threat landscape has become a major task in itself.

☑ When responding to security incidents, analysts are forced to spend a lot of time manually checking and disseminating data from disparate sources.

☑ Containment of attacks and eradication of vulnerabilities continually grows more difficult.

As a result, incident response teams routinely operate under enormous time pressures and often are unable to contain cyber incidents promptly.

Continuing Challenges

While it's difficult to be precise about the number of incidents experienced by a typical organization, there is no doubt that cyberattack volume is growing rapidly. According to SonicWall, the global volume of malware attacks increased by more than 18 percent during 2017 alone. Other popular attack vectors, such as encrypted traffic and phishing, are also seeing substantial increases in volume every year. While some of this growing pressure is mitigated by preventative technologies, a huge additional strain is nonetheless being placed on incident response teams because of the following factors.

A skills gap

Incident response is not an entry-level security function. It encompasses a vast swath of skills, including static and dynamic malware analysis, reverse engineering, digital forensics, and more. It requires analysts who have experience in the industry and can be relied upon to perform complex operations under pressure.

The highly publicized cybersecurity skills gap has grown consistently wider over the past decade. According to a 2017 research report by ISSA, almost three-quarters of security professionals claim their organization is affected by the global skills shortage. In their most recent Global Information Security Workforce Study, Frost & Sullivan predicts the skills gap will grow to 1.8 million workers by 2022.

Too many alerts, too little time

In tandem with the lack of available personnel, incident response teams are bombarded by an unmanageable number of alerts. According to the Ponemon "Cost of Malware Containment" report, security teams can expect to log almost 17,000 malware alerts in a typical week. That's more than 100 alerts per hour for a team that operates 24/7. And those are only the alerts from malware incidents.

To put these figures in perspective, all these alerts can lead security teams to spend over 21,000 man-hours each year chasing down false positives. That's 2,625 standard eight-hour shifts needed just to distinguish bad alerts from good ones.

Time to response is rising

When you have too few skilled personnel and too many alerts, there's only one outcome: the time to resolve genuine security incidents will rise. According to analysis of source data from a recent Verizon Data Breach Investigations Report, while median time to incident detection is a fairly reasonable four hours, median time to resolution (MTTR) is more than four days.

Of course, cybercriminals have no such time constraints. Once they gain a foothold inside a target network, time to compromise is usually measured in minutes. We will discuss this more in Chapter 6.

A piecemeal approach

Most organizations' security groups have grown organically in parallel with increases in cyber risk. As a result, they have added security technologies and processes piecemeal, without a strategic design.

While this ad hoc approach is perfectly normal, it forces incident response teams to spend a lot of time aggregating data and context from a variety of security technologies (e.g., SIEM, EDR, and firewall logs) and threat feeds. This effort significantly extends response times and increases the likelihood that mistakes will be made.

ON THE WEB

You can find the original "Cost of Malware Containment" report on the Ponemon website.

The Reactivity Problem

Once an alert is flagged, it must be triaged, remediated, and followed up as quickly as possible to minimize cyber risk.

Consider a typical incident response process:

1. **Incident detection** — Receive an alert from a SIEM, EDR, or similar product.

2. **Discovery** — Determine what's happened and how to respond.

3. **Triage and containment** — Take immediate actions to mitigate the threat and minimize damage.

4. **Remediation** — Repair damage and remove infections.

5. **Push to BAU** — Pass the incident to "business as usual" teams for final actions.

Notice how reactive this process is. For most organizations, nearly all the work necessary to remediate an incident is back-loaded, meaning it can't be completed until after an alert is flagged. Although this is inevitable to some degree, it is far from ideal when incident response teams are already struggling to resolve incidents quickly enough.

Minimizing Reactivity in Incident Response

To reduce response times, incident response teams must become less reactive. Two areas where advanced preparation can be especially helpful are identification of probable threats and prioritization.

Identification of probable threats

If an incident response team can identify the most commonly faced threats in advance, they can develop strong, consistent processes to cope with them. This preparation dramatically reduces the time the team needs to contain individual incidents, prevents mistakes, and frees up analysts to cope with new and unexpected threats when they arise.

Prioritization

Not all threats are equal. If incident response teams can understand which threat vectors pose the greatest level of risk to their organization, they can allocate their time and resources accordingly.

ON THE WEB

To find out how security experts use threat intelligence to reduce reactivity in incident response, watch the joint Recorded Future and LIFARS webinar "Fuel Incident Response With Threat Intelligence to Lower Breach Impact."

Strengthening Incident Response With Threat Intelligence

It should be clear from our discussion so far that *security technologies by themselves can't do enough to reduce pressure on human analysts.*

Threat intelligence can minimize the pressure on incident response teams and address many of the issues we have been reviewing by:

☑ Automatically identifying and dismissing false positive alerts

☑ Enriching alerts with real-time context from across the open and dark web

☑ Assembling and comparing information from internal and external data sources to identify genuine threats

☑ Scoring threats according to the organization's specific needs and infrastructure

In other words, threat intelligence provides incident response teams with exactly the actionable insights they need to make faster, better decisions, while holding back the tide of irrelevant and unreliable alerts that typically make their job so difficult.

Threat Intelligence in Action

Let's look at three use cases and one abuse case that show how threat intelligence affects incident response teams in the real world.

Use case: Prepare processes in advance

As we noted earlier, typical incident response processes are highly reactive, with most activity happening only after an incident occurs. This extends the time needed to scope and remediate incidents.

Threat intelligence can help incident response teams prepare for threats in advance by providing:

- ☑ A comprehensive, up-to-date picture of the threat landscape
- ☑ Information about popular threat actor tactics, techniques, and procedures (TTPs)
- ☑ Highlights of industry- and area-specific attack trends

Using this intelligence, incident response teams can develop and maintain strong processes for the most common incidents and threats. Having these processes available speeds up incident discovery, triage, and containment. It also greatly improves the consistency and reliability of actions across the incident response function.

Use case: Scope and contain incidents

When an incident occurs, incident response analysts must determine:

1. What happened
2. What the incident might mean for the organization
3. Which actions to take

All three of these factors must be analyzed as quickly as possible with a high degree of accuracy. Threat intelligence can help by:

☑ Automatically dismissing false positives, enabling teams to focus on genuine security incidents

☑ Enriching incidents with related information from across the open and dark web, making it easier to determine how much of a threat they pose and how the organization might be affected

☑ Providing details about the threat and insights about the attacker TTPs, helping the team make fast and effective containment and remediation decisions

Is Time Your Friend or Enemy?

Ever wondered how the balance of power fluctuates between attackers and defenders as time goes by? To find out, read the Recorded Future blog post "The 4th in the 5th: Temporal Aspects of Cyber Operations" by the grugq.

Use case: Remediate data exposure and stolen assets

It's common for organizations to take a long time to realize a breach has occurred. According to the "Ponemon 2018 Cost of a Data Breach Study," organizations in the United States take an average of 196 days to detect a breach.

Not surprisingly, stolen data and proprietary assets often turn up for sale on the dark web before their rightful owners realize what's happened.

A powerful threat intelligence capability can be a tremendous advantage. It can alert you to a breach by providing early warning that:

☑ Your assets are exposed online

☑ Someone is offering your assets for sale

Obtaining this intelligence in real time is vital because it will enable you to contain the incident as quickly as possible and help you identify when and how your network was breached.

Abuse case: Half measures are worse than nothing

We want to caution you about one "abuse case" where threat intelligence can actually undermine incident response.

At the start of their threat intelligence journey, some organizations opt for a minimalist solution such as a threat intelligence solution paired with a variety of free threat feeds. They might believe that this "dip the toes in the water" approach will minimize up-front costs.

While this type of implementation arms incident response teams with some actionable intelligence, it usually makes things worse by forcing analysts to wade through vast quantities of false positives and irrelevant alerts. To fully address the primary incident response pain points, a threat intelligence capability must be comprehensive, relevant, contextualized, and integrated.

Essential Characteristics of Threat Intelligence for Incident Response

Now it's time for us to examine the characteristics of a powerful threat intelligence capability, and how they address the greatest pain points of incident response teams.

Comprehensive

To be valuable to incident response teams, threat intelligence must be captured automatically from the widest possible range of locations across open sources, technical feeds, and the dark web. Otherwise analysts will be forced to conduct their own manual research to ensure nothing important has been missed.

TECH TALK

Imagine an analyst needs to know whether an IP address has been associated with malicious activity. If she is confident that her threat intelligence has been drawn from a comprehensive range of threat sources, she can query the data instantly and be sure the result will be accurate. If she isn't confident, she will have to spend time manually checking the IP address against several threat data sources. Figure 4-1 shows how threat intelligence might connect an IP address with the Trickbot malware. This kind of intelligence can be correlated with internal network logs to reveal indicators of compromise.

Figure 4-1: Threat intelligence connecting an IP address with the Trickbot malware. (Source: Recorded Future)

ON THE WEB While they are often used interchangeably, threat intelligence, information, and data aren't the same thing. To find out where the differences lie, read the Recorded Future blog post "Threat Intelligence, Information, and Data: What Is the Difference?"

Relevant

It's impossible to avoid all false positives when working to identify and contain incidents. But threat intelligence should help incident response teams quickly identify and purge false positives generated by security technologies such as SIEM and EDR products.

There are two categories of false positives to consider:

1. Alerts that are relevant to an organization but are inaccurate or unhelpful

2. Alerts that are accurate and/or interesting but *aren't* relevant to the organization

Both types have the potential to waste an enormous amount of incident response analysts' time.

Advanced threat intelligence products are now employing machine learning technology to identify and discard false positives automatically and draw analysts' attention to the most important (i.e., most relevant) intelligence.

CAUTION

If you don't choose your threat intelligence technology carefully, your team can waste a great deal of time on intelligence that's inaccurate, outdated, or irrelevant to your organization.

Contextualized

Not all threats are created equal. Even among relevant threat alerts, some will inevitably be more urgent and important than the rest. An alert from a single source could be both accurate and relevant, but still not particularly high in priority. That is why context is so important: it provides critical clues about which alerts are most likely to be significant to your organization.

Contextual information related to an alert might include:

☑ Corroboration from multiple sources that the same type of alert has been associated with recent attacks

☑ Confirmation that it has been associated with threat actors known to be active in your industry

☑ A timeline showing that the alert occurred slightly before or after other events linked with attacks

Modern machine learning and artificial intelligence (AI) technologies make it possible for a threat intelligence solution to consider multiple sources concurrently and determine which alerts are most important to a specific organization.

Integrated

Among the most critical functions of a threat intelligence system is the ability to integrate with a broad range of security tools, including SIEM and incident response solutions, examine the alerts they generate, and:

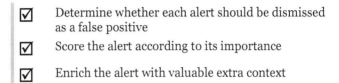

- ☑ Determine whether each alert should be dismissed as a false positive
- ☑ Score the alert according to its importance
- ☑ Enrich the alert with valuable extra context

This integration eliminates the need for analysts to manually compare each alert to information in diverse security and threat intelligence tools. Even more important, integration and automated processes can filter out a huge number of false positives *without any checking by a human analyst*. The amount of time and frustration this capability saves makes it perhaps the single greatest benefit of threat intelligence for incident response teams.

Chapter 5

Threat Intelligence for Vulnerability Management

In this chapter

- Examine the current challenges in addressing vulnerabilities based on actual risk
- Learn how vulnerability intelligence delivers insights into threat actor behaviors
- See how risk-based intelligence streamlines the operational elements of vulnerability management

"The acknowledgment of our weakness is the first step in repairing our loss."

— Thomas à Kempis

Vulnerability management is not glamorous, but it is one of the very few ways you can be proactive in securing your organization. Its importance as a function cannot be overstated.

The key to success in vulnerability management is to shift the thinking of your security teams from trying to patch everything to making risk-based decisions. That is critical because the vast ocean of vulnerabilities disclosed each year stretches to the breaking point the teams responsible for identifying vulnerable assets and deploying patches. And the key to making good risk-based decisions is taking advantage of more sources of threat intelligence.

The Vulnerability Problem by the Numbers

According to research from the analyst firm Gartner, Inc., about 8,000 vulnerabilities a year were disclosed over the past decade. The number rose only slightly from year to year, and only about one in eight were actually exploited. However, during the same period, the amount of new software coming into use grew immensely, and the number of threats has increased exponentially.

In other words, although the number of breaches and threats has increased over the past 10 years, only a small percentage were based on new vulnerabilities. As Gartner put it, "More threats are leveraging the same small set of vulnerabilities."

Zero day does not mean top priority

Zero-day threats regularly draw an outsize amount of attention. However, the vast majority of "new" threats labeled as zero day are actually variations on a theme, exploiting the same old vulnerabilities in slightly different ways. Further, the data shows that the number of vulnerabilities actually exploited on day zero make up only about 0.4 percent of all vulnerabilities exploited during the last decade.

The implication is that the most effective approach to vulnerability management is not to focus on zero-day threats, but rather to identify and patch the vulnerabilities specific to the software your organization uses.

Time is of the essence

Threat actors have gotten quicker at exploiting vulnerabilities. According to Gartner, the average time it takes between the identification of a vulnerability and the appearance of an exploit in the wild has dropped from 45 days to 15 days over the last decade.

This has two implications:

1. You have roughly two weeks to patch or remediate your systems against a new exploit.
2. If you can't patch in that timeframe, you should have a plan to mitigate the damage.

Research from IBM X-Force shows that if a vulnerability is not exploited within two weeks to three months after it is announced, it is statistically unlikely that it ever will be. Therefore "old" vulnerabilities are usually not a priority for patching.

 ON THE WEB Exploits usually target the most widely used technologies. An episode of the Recorded Future podcast entitled "7 of the Top 10 Vulnerabilities Target Microsoft" explains why.

 DON'T FORGET All of these statistics point to one conclusion: your goal should not be to patch the most vulnerabilities, or even the most zero-day threats, but rather to identify and address the threats most likely to be exploited against your organization.

Assess Risk Based on Exploitability

Let's use a metaphor: if patching vulnerabilities to keep your network safe is like getting vaccines to protect yourself from disease, then you need to decide which vaccinations are priorities and which are unnecessary. You may need a flu shot every season to stay healthy, but there's no need to stay vaccinated against yellow fever or malaria unless you will be exposed to them.

That's why you have to do your research: one of the greatest values of a threat intelligence solution is that it identifies the specific vulnerabilities that represent risk to your organization and gives you visibility into their likelihood of exploitation.

Figure 5-1 illustrates the point. Out of the thousands of vulnerabilities that are currently disclosed, hundreds are being exploited. And it's true that at least some of those vulnerabilities probably exist in your environment. But the only ones you really need to worry about are those that lie within the intersection of those two categories.

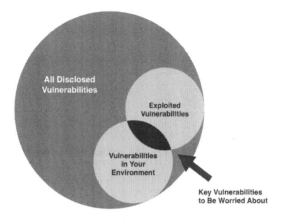

Figure 5-1: The biggest risks are vulnerabilities that are present in your organization and currently being exploited. (Source: Gartner)

Severity ratings can be misleading

A common mistake in managing vulnerabilities is to focus on ranking threats in terms of severity. Ranking and classification systems like Common Vulnerabilities and Exposures (CVE) naming and Common Vulnerability Scoring Systems (CVSSs) don't take into account whether threat actors are actually exploiting vulnerabilities right now in your industry or locations. Relying solely on vulnerability severity is like getting a vaccine for the bubonic plague before a flu shot because the plague killed more people at some point in history.

The Genesis of Threat Intelligence: Vulnerability Databases

Vulnerability databases consolidate information on disclosed vulnerabilities and also score their exploitability.

In fact, one of the very first forms of threat intelligence was NIST's National Vulnerability Database (NVD). It centralized information on disclosed vulnerabilities to help make it easier for organizations to see if they were likely to be affected. For more than 20 years, the NVD has collected information on more than 100,000 vulnerabilities, making it an invaluable source for information security professionals. Other nations, including China and Russia, have followed NIST's lead by setting up vulnerability databases.

ON THE WEB

You can find the NIST NVD at https://nvd.nist.gov/. A catalog of vulnerability databases is published by the industry organization FIRST: https://www.first.org/global/sigs/vrdx/vdb-catalog.

However, there are two significant limitations to most vulnerability databases:

1. They focus on technical exploitability rather than active exploitation.

2. They are not updated fast enough to provide warning of some quickly spreading threats.

Exploitability versus exploitation

Information in the vulnerability databases is almost entirely focused on technical exploitability, a judgment of how likely it is that exploiting a particular vulnerability will result in greater or lesser damage to systems and networks. In the NVD, this is measured through the CVSS scoring system.

But technical exploitability and active exploitation are not the same thing. CVSS base scores provide a metric that's reasonably accurate and easy to understand — provided you know what information the score is conveying. But unless a base score is modified by a temporal score or an environmental score, it really only tells you how bad the vulnerability is *hypothetically*, not whether it's actually being exploited in the wild.

Figure 5-2 shows the kind of threat intelligence available about a vulnerability and the risk it poses. In this case you can also see how reports involving the CVE are appearing before it has been given a CVSS score by NVD.

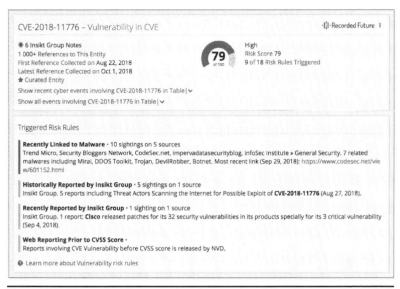

Figure 5-2: Threat intelligence related to a vulnerability. (Source: Recorded Future)

TECH TALK

An object lesson in the difference between the NVD's "official risk" and "real risk" from a vulnerability in the wild is CVE-2017-0022. Despite its having a CVSS severity score of only 4.3 (in the medium range), Recorded Future recently included it in a list of the top 10 vulnerabilities used by cybercriminals. The real risk is very high because threat actors have added this vulnerability to the widespread Neutrino Exploit Kit, where it performs a critical role checking whether security software is installed on a target system.

Next week versus now

Another shortcoming of many vulnerability databases is lack of timeliness. For example, 75 percent of disclosed vulnerabilities appear on other online sources before they appear in the NVD, and on average it takes those vulnerabilities a week to show up there. This is a very serious problem, because it handicaps security teams in the race to patch before adversaries can exploit, as illustrated in Figure 5-3.

TECH TALK

The informal way in which vulnerabilities are disclosed and announced contributes to the delay in recognizing them in vulnerability databases. Typically, a vendor or researcher discloses the vulnerability to the NVD, which assigns a CVE and begins an analysis. In the meantime, the vendor or researcher publishes more information on its own blog or a social media account. Good luck collating data from these disparate and hard-to-find sources before criminal actors develop proof-of-concept malware and add it to exploit kits!

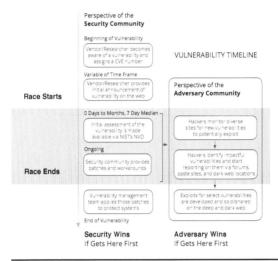

Figure 5-3: The race between security professionals and adversaries.

ON THE WEB

For research on the lag in reporting vulnerabilities and its implications, see the Recorded Future blog post "The Race Between Security Professionals and Adversaries."

Threat Intelligence and Real Risk

The most effective way to assess the true risk of a vulnerability to your organization is to combine:

- ☑ Internal vulnerability scanning data

- ☑ External intelligence from a breadth of sources

- ☑ An understanding of why threat actors are targeting certain vulnerabilities and ignoring others

Internal vulnerability scanning

Almost every vulnerability management team scans their internal systems for vulnerabilities, correlates the results with information reported in vulnerability databases, and uses the result to determine what should be patched. This is a basic use of operational threat intelligence, even if we don't usually think of it that way.

Conventional scanning is an excellent way to *de-prioritize* vulnerabilities that don't appear on your systems. By itself, however, scanning is not an adequate way to accurately prioritize vulnerabilities that are found.

Risk milestones for vulnerabilities

One powerful way to assess the risk of a vulnerability is to look at how far it has progressed from initial identification to availability, weaponization, and commoditization in exploit kits.

The level of real risk rises dramatically as it passes through the milestones shown in Figure 5-4. Broad-based threat intelligence can reveal the progress of a vulnerability along this path.

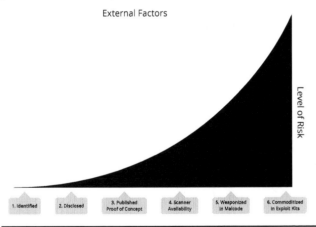

Figure 5-4: Real risk rises dramatically when vulnerabilities progress to weaponization and commoditization.

Understanding the adversary

As discussed elsewhere in this book, good threat intelligence should not simply provide information in the form of scores and statistics, but also a deeper understanding of how and why threat actors are targeting certain vulnerabilities and ignoring others. Below we discuss sources of intelligence that can contribute to this understanding.

How to Create Meaningful Risk Scores

What factors beyond technical characteristics can be used to calculate risk scores of vulnerabilities? Recorded Future's native risk scoring system incorporates data about criminal adoption, patterns in exploit sharing, and the number of links to malware. This information often comes from sources that are difficult to access, like forums on the dark web.

Sources of Intelligence

Data from asset scans and external vulnerability databases are only the starting points for information that can help you assess the risk of vulnerabilities. Threat intelligence should include data from a wide range of sources, or analysts risk missing emerging vulnerabilities until it's too late.

Valuable sources of information for assessing true risk to your business include:

- ☑ **Information security sites**, including vendor blogs, official disclosure information on vulnerabilities, and security news sites
- ☑ **Social media**, where link sharing provides jumping-off points for uncovering useful intelligence
- ☑ **Code repositories** such as GitHub, which yield insights into the development of proof-of-concept code for vulnerabilities
- ☑ **Paste sites** such as Pastebin and Ghostbin (sometimes wrongly defined as dark web locations), which often house lists of exploitable vulnerabilities
- ☑ **The dark web**, composed of communities and marketplaces with a bar to entry where exploits are developed, shared, and sold

☑ **Forums** with no bar to entry or requirement to be using specific software, where threat actors exchange information on vulnerabilities and exploits

☑ **Technical feeds**, which deliver data streams of potentially malicious indicators that add useful context around the activities of malware and exploit kits

Vulnerability Chatter on the Dark Web

It's not easy to eavesdrop on the channels through which threat actors communicate and operate:

- Underground forums are difficult to find (after all, there's no Google for the dark web).

- Threat actors change locations whenever they feel their anonymity is at risk.

- Finding the crumb that might be relevant to your security is no small endeavor.

- There are likely to be bars to entry, either financial or kudos from the rest of the community.

- Many of these forums operate exclusively in local languages.

Threat intelligence vendors with expertise in collecting and analyzing dark web intelligence come into play here. They can provide you with contextualized information from dark web forums on vulnerabilities directly relevant to your network.

Figure 5-5: A post in a dark web forum shows threat actors exchanging information. (Source: Recorded Future)

Use Case: Cross-Referencing Intelligence

To accurately assess real risk, you must be able to correlate information from multiple threat intelligence sources. Once you begin to understand how individual references combine to tell the whole story, you will be able to map the intelligence you have to the risk milestones a vulnerability typically goes through.

For example, you might notice a new vulnerability disclosed on a vendor's website. Then you discover a tweet with a link to proof-of-concept code on GitHub. Later you find exploit code is being sold on a dark web forum. Eventually you might see news reports of the vulnerability being exploited in the wild.

 This kind of intelligence can help you narrow your focus to vulnerabilities that truly present the greatest risk and move away from a "race to patch everything" mode of operation.

Bridging the Risk Gaps Between Security, Operations, and Business Leadership

In most organizations, the responsibility for protecting against vulnerabilities devolves onto two teams:

1. The vulnerability management team runs scans and prioritizes vulnerabilities by potential risk.
2. The IT operations team deploys patches and remediates the affected systems.

This dynamic creates a tendency to approach vulnerability management "by the numbers." For example, the vulnerability management team in the security organization might determine that several vulnerabilities in Apache web servers pose a very high risk to the business and should be given top priority. However, the IT operations team may be supporting a lot more Windows systems than Apache servers. If team members are measured strictly on the number of systems patched, they have an incentive to keep their focus on lower-priority Windows vulnerabilities.

Intelligence on exploitability also prepares your organization to strike the correct balance between patching vulnerable systems and interrupting business operations. Most organizations have a strong aversion to disturbing business continuity. But if you know that a patch will protect the organization against a real, imminent risk, then a short interruption is completely justified.

The risk milestones framework outlined above makes it much easier to communicate the danger of a vulnerability across your security and operations teams, up through senior managers, and even to the board. This level of visibility into the rationale behind decisions made around vulnerabilities will increase confidence in the security team across your entire organization.

 TIP
To reduce the gap between the vulnerability management and IT operations teams, introduce risk of exploitability. Arm the vulnerability management team with more contextualized data about the risk of exploitability so they can pinpoint a smaller number of high-risk CVEs and make fewer demands on the operations team. The operations team can then give first priority to that small number of critical patches and still have time to address other goals.

Chapter 6

Threat Intelligence for Security Leaders

- See how threat intelligence supports risk management and targeted investment in cybersecurity programs
- Explore the types of threat intelligence CISOs find most valuable
- Review how threat intelligence helps mitigate the security skills gap

"An investment in knowledge pays the best interest."

– Benjamin Franklin

The job of the CISO has seen dramatic shifts in recent years. It once centered on making decisions about purchasing and implementing security technologies. Now CISOs are far more likely to interact with the CEO and the board and to perform delicate balancing acts of pre-empting risk while ensuring business continuity.

Today, security leaders must:

- ☑ Assess business and technical risks, including emerging threats and "known unknowns" that might impact the business
- ☑ Identify the right strategies and technologies to mitigate the risks
- ☑ Communicate the nature of the risks to top management and justify investments in defensive measures

Threat intelligence can be a critical resource for all these activities.

Risk Management

Perhaps the greatest responsibility of the modern CISO is risk management: taking the resources and budget available and allocating them in a way that most efficiently mitigates the threat of cyber incidents and attacks. Figure 6-1 outlines the stages security leaders move through when approaching this challenge.

Assess Security Requirements	Understand business and IT objectives and define responsibilities for the security function.
Assess Existing Security Protocols	Analyze current security people, processes, and technologies to develop an accurate picture of the security function.
Develop Initiatives	Using a risk-based approach, identify the most significant gaps in security, then define and prioritize initiatives to address them.
Plan the Transition	Continually monitor progress and ensure the security function is improving in line with requirements. Develop metrics to measure ongoing effectiveness.

Figure 6-1: A standard approach to assessing risk and developing a security strategy.

Internal data is not enough

The approach to security outlined in Figure 6-1 depends on having good information about relevant risk factors and potential weaknesses in existing security programs. The problem is that too often this kind of intelligence is only gathered from internal audits, known issues, and previous security incidents. That produces a list of problems you already know about, not a list of the problems you need to worry about today or in the future.

External context is needed to verify risk related to known problems and provide warning about emerging and unforeseen threats.

Internal network traffic data, event logs, and alerting obviously bring value to risk management, but they don't provide enough context to build a comprehensive risk profile, and certainly not enough to define an entire strategy. Security professionals must be proactive about uncovering unknown risks. Context is what helps security leaders determine which potential threats are most likely to become actual threats to their enterprise.

Sharpening the focus

Threat intelligence includes information on general trends such as:

- ☑ Which types of attacks are becoming more (or less) frequent
- ☑ Which types of attacks are most costly to the victims
- ☑ What new kinds of threat actors are coming forward, and which assets and enterprises are they targeting
- ☑ The security practices and technologies that have proven the most (or least) successful in stopping or mitigating these attacks

Data on these trends can help security organizations antici-pate which threats will be the hot news items of tomorrow.

But contextualized external threat intelligence can go much further, enabling security groups to assess whether an emerg-ing threat is likely to affect their specific enterprise based on factors like:

- ☑ **Industry**: Is the threat affecting other businesses in our vertical?
- ☑ **Technology**: Does the threat involve compromis-ing software, hardware, or other technologies used in our enterprise?
- ☑ **Geography**: Does the threat target facilities in regions where we have operations?
- ☑ **Attack method**: Have techniques used in the attack, including social engineering and technical methods, been used successfully against our com-pany or similar ones?

Without these types of intelligence, gathered from an extremely broad set of external data sources, it is impossible for security decision makers to obtain a holistic view of the cyber risk landscape and the greatest risks to their enterprise.

Figure 6-2 illustrates how a customized threat intelligence dashboard can highlight intelligence that is most relevant to a specific enterprise.

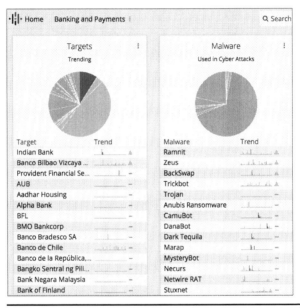

Figure 6-2: A threat intelligence dashboard can pinpoint threats most relevant to a specific industry or technology. (Source: Recorded Future)

Mitigation: People, Processes, and Tools

Vulnerability scans and techniques such as penetration testing and red teaming can help security organizations understand where gaps exist in their defenses.

But today's enterprises have far more technical vulnerabilities, more weaknesses in security processes and policies, and more employees susceptible to social engineering techniques than they can possibly patch, harden, and train in the immediate future.

Threat intelligence helps security leaders pinpoint the vulner-abilities and weaknesses that need to be addressed first by indicating:

- ☑ Which threat actors are most likely to target the enterprise
- ☑ The TTPs those threat actors use, and therefore the weaknesses they tend to exploit

Early warnings

Sometimes threat intelligence can be even more specific. For example, analysts have found hackers on the dark web announcing their intention to attack specific industries, and even specific companies (sometimes to recruit like-minded hackers to assist them).

Analysts monitoring dark web marketplaces can also track the development and sale of hacker tools and exploit kits targeting specific vulnerabilities. As discussed earlier in this book, it is important to patch vulnerabilities and mitigate weaknesses that are at the point of being exploited before tackling others where exploitation is theoretical.

TIP You can use some threat intelligence solutions to scan the dark web and other sources for references to your company, your industry, and specific technologies installed in your enterprise.

Investment

Deciding how to invest in cybersecurity has become a daunt-ing challenge in recent times. Financial investment advisers Momentum Partners identified more than 1,700 companies in 2017 that specialize in cybersecurity technologies and services. With so many choices, how can CISOs identify the most effective solutions to implement as part of a proactive security strategy?

The only logical way is to make investment decisions based on risk. Each organization has its own unique risk profile, shaped by its industry, locations, and internal infrastructure. Threat intelligence helps security leaders understand their organization's most pressing threats, making the task of identifying (and justifying) areas for investment much simpler. The end goal is to be able to judge that risk and make investments based upon sound knowledge of the true threat landscape.

Communication

CISOs are often challenged by the need to describe threats and justify countermeasures in terms that will motivate non-technical business leaders, such as cost, ROI, impact on customers, and competitive advantages.

Bombarding them with news about every single threat is not a good option.

Threat intelligence can provide powerful ammunition for these discussions, such as:

☑ The impact of similar attacks on companies of the same size in other industries

☑ Trends and intelligence from the dark web indicating that the enterprise is likely to be targeted

Supporting Security Leaders

We have mentioned several times that threat intelligence needs to be comprehensive, relevant, and contextualized to be useful to members of the security organization. When it comes to CISOs and other security leaders, it also needs to be concise and timely.

For example, threat intelligence can provide security leaders with a real-time picture of the latest threats, trends, and events. A threat intelligence dashboard or some other type of "at-a-glance" format can help security leaders respond to a threat or communicate the potential impact of a new threat type to business leaders and board members.

DON'T FORGET

Threat intelligence is not just for incident response teams and SOCs. Security leaders are also key consumers of threat intelligence, as illustrated in Figure 2-1. Think through the kinds of intelligence security leaders need on a daily basis (say, a dashboard and a list of key new intelligence findings from the previous day), at regular intervals (summaries and trends for a quarterly risk report), and for crises (intelligence about attacks that have just been detected), and make sure processes and threat intelligence tools are in place to address these needs.

The Security Skills Gap

One of the responsibilities of a CISO is to make sure the IT organization has the human resources to carry out its mission. Yet the cybersecurity field has a widely publicized skills shortage, and existing security staff frequently find themselves under pressure to cope with unmanageable workloads.

Threat intelligence can provide a partial answer to that crisis by automating some of the most labor-intensive tasks in cybersecurity and freeing people's time for other tasks. For example, it can reduce the massive volume of alerts generated by SIEMs and other security tools, rapidly collect and correlate context from multiple intelligence sources, and provide data to prioritize risks.

A threat intelligence solution made available across the security function can save a huge amount of time, as SOC and incident response analysts, vulnerability management specialists, and other security personnel are given the information and context they need to make accurate decisions.

Powerful threat intelligence also helps junior personnel quickly "upskill" and perform above their experience level, so the CISO doesn't have to recruit as many senior staff.

Intelligence to Manage Better

It's clear that the greatest challenge for CISOs and other security leaders is how to balance limited resources against the need to secure their organizations against ever-evolving cyber threats. Threat intelligence addresses these issues by helping them to build a picture of the threat landscape, accurately calculate cyber risk, and arm security personnel with the intelligence and context they need to make better, faster decisions.

Threat intelligence enables CISOs and security leaders to stay abreast of current and emerging threats in a way that simply isn't possible through manual research. But for that to happen, a threat intelligence capability must be comprehensive, relevant, contextualized, concise, and timely. Threat intelligence capabilities without these characteristics will most likely hinder more than help, as partial or inaccurate information can easily lead to poor decision making.

Case Study: Threat Intelligence and Automation at a Global Retailer

With nearly 3,600 stores and over 135,000 employees worldwide, the chain's security challenges run the gamut from loss prevention, fraud, and corporate security to protecting customers' PII.

The retailer applies automation to both centralizing and customizing threat intelligence for every security function. Automation ensures that data going into its SIEM is accurate and highly contextual, and that the data coming out is in flexible, easy-to-use formats.

The biggest return on investment — and the biggest advantage to managing its threat intelligence through an all-in-one platform — is better relationships both across the cybersecurity teams and with other departments in the organization.

Says a senior manager at the company's Cyber Defense Center: "None of us is operating in a silo. If we can use threat intelligence to keep us safe, but also help our program visibility, that helps to make a business case for more capabilities. Having champions on other teams to back the benefits of threat intelligence really helps our return on investment."

Read the full case study or watch the webinar at https://www.recordedfuture.com/gap-threat-intelligence-needs/.

Chapter 7

Threat Intelligence for Risk Analysis

- Explore the value of risk models like the FAIR framework
- See right and wrong ways to gather data about risk
- Learn how threat intelligence can provide hard data about attack probabilities and costs

"Establish and promote information risk management best practices that ...[achieve] the right balance between protecting the organization and running the business."

— Mission statement of the FAIR Institute

A s we mentioned in the previous chapter, today there are more than 1,700 vendors in cybersecurity. Most of them define their mission as some version of "making your environment secure." But how can enterprises set priorities for investing in technology and services, as well as people?

Risk modeling offers a way to objectively assess current risks, and to estimate clear and quantifiable outcomes from investments in cybersecurity. But many cyber risk models today suffer from either:

☑ Vague, non-quantified output, often in the form of "stoplight charts" that show green, yellow, and red threat levels

☑ Estimates about threat probabilities and costs that are hastily compiled, based on partial information, and riddled with unfounded assumptions

Non-quantified output is not very actionable, while models based on faulty input result in "garbage in-garbage out" scenarios, whose output appears to be precise but is in fact misleading.

To avoid these problems, enterprises need a well-designed risk model and plenty of valid, current information, including threat intelligence.

Cybersecurity risk assessments should not be based only on criteria defined to prove compliance with regulations. With those criteria, assessing risk usually becomes an exercise in checking boxes against cybersecurity controls like firewalls and encryption. Counting the number of boxes checked gives you a very misleading picture of actual risk.

The FAIR Risk Model

The type of equation at the core of any risk model is:

"Likelihood of occurrence x impact"

But clearly God (or the Devil) is in the details. Fortunately, some smart people have developed some very good risk models and methodologies that you can use or adapt to your own needs. One that we like is the Factor Analysis of Information Risk (FAIR) model from the FAIR Institute. Figure 7-1 shows the framework of this model.

The FAIR framework helps you create a quantitative risk assessment model that contains specific probabilities for loss from specific kinds of threats.

You can learn more about FAIR at the FAIR Institute website. This quantitative model for information security and operational risk is focused on understanding, analyzing, and quantifying information risk in real financial terms.

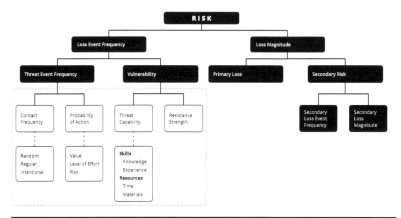

Figure 7-1: The FAIR Framework, with elements informed by intelligence highlighted. (Source: The FAIR Institute)

Measurements and transparency are key

The FAIR framework (and others like it) enable you to create risk models that:

☑ Make defined measurements of risk

☑ Are transparent about assumptions, variables, and outcomes

☑ Show specific loss probabilities in financial terms

When measurements, formulas, assumptions, variables, and outcomes are made transparent, they can be discussed, defended, and changed. Because much of the FAIR model is defined in business and financial terms, executives, line of business managers, and other stakeholders can learn to speak the same language and to classify assets, threats, and vulnerabilities in the same way.

TIP Try to incorporate specific probabilities about future losses into your risk model whenever possible. Specific probabilities enable risk managers and senior executives to discuss the model and how it can be improved, after which they have more confidence in the model and the recommendations that come out of it.

Which Statement Is More Useful?

"The threat from DDoS attacks to our business has been changed from high to medium (red to yellow)."

Or

"There is a 20 percent probability that our business will incur a loss of over $300,000 in the next 12 months because a distributed denial-of-service (DDoS) attack will disrupt the availability of our customer-facing websites."

"The threat of ransomware to our business has changed from low to medium (green to yellow)."

Or

"There is a 10 percent probability that our business will incur a loss of $150,000 in the next 12 months due to ransomware."

Threat Intelligence and Threat Probabilities

As shown in the left side of Figure 7-1, a big part of creating a threat model involves estimating the probability of successful attacks (or "loss event frequency" in the language of the FAIR framework).

The first step is to create a list of threat categories that might affect the business. This list typically includes malware, phishing attacks, exploit kits, zero-day attacks, web application exploits, DDoS attacks, ransomware, and many other threats.

The next step is much more difficult: to estimate probabilities that the attacks will happen, and that they will succeed (i.e., the odds that the enterprise contains vulnerabilities related to the attacks and existing controls are not sufficient to stop them).

 Try to avoid the following scenario: A GRC (governance, risk, and compliance) team member asks a security analyst, "What is the likelihood of our facing this particular attack?" The security analyst (who really can't win) thinks for 30 seconds about past experience and current security controls and makes a wild guess: "I dunno, maybe 20 percent."

To avoid appearing clueless, your security team needs answers that are better informed than that one. Threat intelligence can help by answering questions such as:

- ☑ Which threat actors are using this attack, and do they target our industry?
- ☑ How often has this specific attack been observed recently by enterprises like ours?
- ☑ Is the trend up or down?
- ☑ Which vulnerabilities does this attack exploit (and are those vulnerabilities present in our enterprise)?
- ☑ What kind of damage, technical and financial, has this attack caused in enterprises like ours?

Analysts still need to know a great deal about the enterprise and its security defenses, but threat intelligence enriches their knowledge of attacks, the actors behind them, and their targets. It also provides hard data on the prevalence of the attacks.

Figures 7-2 and 7-3 show some of the forms the intelligence might take. Figure 7-2 lists the kinds of questions about a malware sample that a threat intelligence solution can answer for analysts.

Figure 7-2: Questions about a malware sample that a threat intelligence solution can answer. (Source: Recorded Future)

Figure 7-3 shows trends in the proliferation of ransomware families. The trend line to the right of each ransomware family indicates increasing or decreasing references across a huge range of threat data sources such as code repositories, paste sites, security research blogs, criminal forums, and .onion (Tor accessible) forums. Additional information might be available about how the ransomware families connect to threat actors, targets, and exploit kits.

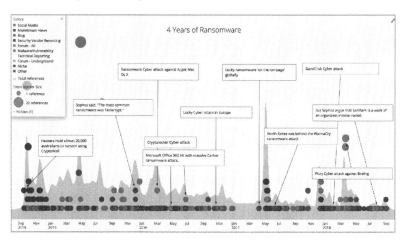

Figure 7-3: Timeline depicting the proliferation of new ransomware families. (Source: Recorded Future)

Threat Intelligence and the Cost of Attacks

The other major component of the formulas in our model is the probable cost of successful attacks. Most of the data for estimating cost is likely to come from inside the enterprise. However, threat intelligence can provide useful reference points on topics like:

- ☑ The cost of similar attacks on enterprises of the same size and in the same industry
- ☑ The systems that need to be remediated after an attack, and the type of remediation they require

Go Deeper on Risk

You can find out more about risk modeling and the role of threat intelligence by viewing the Recorded Future white paper "The Probability of Loss: How Threat Intelligence Quantifies Risk for the Business."

To go even deeper, we highly recommend "How to Measure Anything in Cybersecurity Risk" by Douglas W. Hubbard and Richard Seiersen.

Chapter 8

Threat Intelligence for Fraud Prevention

In this chapter

- Understand how cybercriminals organize themselves to execute fraud and extortion
- See how conversations in criminal communities present opportunities to gather valuable threat intelligence
- Learn which types of cyber fraud you can combat by applying relevant threat intelligence

"The challenge for capitalism is that the things that breed trust also breed the environment for fraud."

— James Surowiecki

Stand and Deliver!

Since the birth of commerce, criminals have looked for ways to make an easy profit from those in possession of assets and to make the most of technology available at the time. In 17th century England, for example, the growth in coach travel among an affluent merchant class, combined with the invention of the portable flintlock pistol, gave rise to the highwayman.

In our digital age, companies that transact business online find their data targeted by various forms of cyber fraud.

To understand how criminals are looking to profit from your business, you cannot focus solely on detecting and responding to threats already actively exploiting your systems. You need to gather threat intelligence about the cybercriminal gangs targeting you and how they run their operations.

Know Your Enemy

Verizon's 2018 Data Breach Investigations Report attributed more than 60 percent of confirmed breaches to organized crime (Figure 8-1).

This data aligns with intelligence gathered by Recorded Future from dark web communities showing that organized criminal groups (OCGs) are employing freelance hackers to defraud businesses and individuals. These groups operate just like legitimate businesses in many ways, with a hierarchy of members working as a team to create, operate, and maintain fraud schemes.

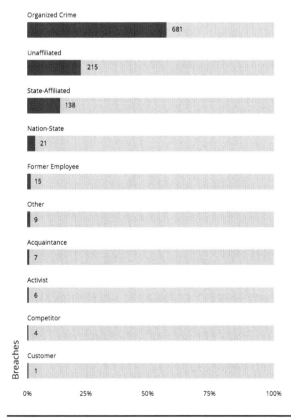

Figure 8-1: Top external actor varieties in data breaches. (Source: Verizon Data Breach Investigation Report 2018)

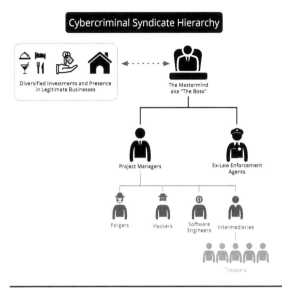

Figure 8-2: A typical organizational chart for a cybercrime syndicate. (Source: Recorded Future)

A typical OCG is controlled by a single mastermind. The group might include bankers with extensive connections in the financial industry to arrange money laundering, forgers responsible for fake documents and supporting paperwork, professional project managers who oversee the technical aspects of operations, software engineers who write code, and skilled hackers. Some groups include ex-law enforcement agents who gather information and run counterintelligence operations.

The members of these cybercriminal syndicates tend to have strong ties in real life, and often they are respected members of their social groups. They certainly don't regard themselves as ordinary street criminals. They rarely cross paths with everyday gangsters, preferring to remain in the shadows and avoid attention from law enforcement and local mafia branches. However, schemes that require large numbers of people, such as those that involve taking cash out of multiple automated teller machines simultaneously, can involve a chain of intermediaries who recruit and manage the "troopers" who do the leg work.

Criminal Communities and the Dark Web

Only rarely can you attribute a cyberattack to a single individual operating in isolation. Advanced attacks typically require a wide range of skills and tools, and an infrastructure capable of launching and supporting campaigns that utilize ransomware, phishing, and other technical devices and social engineering techniques.

Today, all those products and services can be purchased or rented for a price in a sophisticated underground economy. Cybercriminals, hackers, and their accomplices exchange information and carry out transactions related to illicit activities on the deep web (areas of the web that cannot be reached by search engines) and the dark web (areas that can only be accessed with special software and tools that mask the identity of visitors).

Gated communities

Not all cybercriminals operate exclusively in what would technically be referred to as the dark web. Some build communities based on a fairly standard discussion board, encrypted behind a login, and use technologies like Jabber and Telegram to conduct their business.

Prospective members of this underground network are vetted by active participants in the chat rooms and forums before they are accepted. They may have to pay an entrance fee, ranging from US$50 to $2,000 or more. One forum required prospective members to deposit over $100,000.

A strength — and a weakness

The dark web and criminal communities strengthen cybercriminals and OCGs by giving them access to information, tools, infrastructure, and contract services that multiply their power and reach. However, these communities are also a weakness because they can be monitored to provide threat intelligence that can be used to anticipate and defeat fraud schemes.

Know Your Dark Networks

You can gain a deeper under-standing of how the criminal underground maintains a hierarchy of users in research from Recorded Future: "Dark Networks: Social Network Analysis of Dark Web Communities." We found that the dark web is organized in three distinct communities: low-tier underground forums, higher-tier dark web forums, and dark web markets. Analysis revealed that a significant group of actors are posting in both low-tier and higher-tier forums, showing a connection between these two communities. However, dark web markets are largely disconnected from these forums.

Connecting the Dots for Fraud Prevention

Threat intelligence gathered from underground criminal communities is a window into the motivations, methods, and tactics of threat actors, especially when this intelligence is correlated with information from the surface web, including technical feeds and indicators.

The power of truly contextualized threat intelligence is shown by how it can draw together data from a wide variety of sources and make connections between disparate pieces of information.

For example, the following contextual information might be used to turn news about a new malware variant into intelligence:

- ☑ Evidence that criminal groups are using this malware in the wild
- ☑ Reports that exploit kits using the malware are available for sale on the dark web
- ☑ Confirmation that vulnerabilities targeted by the exploit kits are present in your enterprise

TIP Monitor the dark web and criminal communities for direct mentions of your organization and assets. These mentions often indicate targeting or potential breaches. But also monitor mentions of your industry and other less specific terms that might point to your operations. Using threat intelligence to assess risk in this way will give you more confidence about your defenses and help you make better decisions.

Use case: Payment fraud

The term payment fraud encompasses a wide variety of techniques by which cybercriminals profit from compromised payment data. They can use phishing to collect card details. More-complex attacks can compromise ecommerce sites or point-of-sale systems to achieve the same goal. Once they have acquired card data, the criminals can resell it (often as packs of numbers) and walk away with their cut.

Threat intelligence can provide early warning of upcoming attacks related to payment fraud. Monitoring sources like criminal communities, paste sites, and other forums for relevant payment card numbers, bank identifier numbers, or specific references to financial institutions can give visibility into criminal operations that might affect your organization.

Use case: Compromised data

Other types of compromised personal information and corporate intellectual property also can have enormous intrinsic value. Recent examples include compromised medical records, cloned and compromised gift cards, and stolen credentials to "pay for" services like Netflix, Uber, and items charged via PayPal, as illustrated in Figure 8-3.

Figure 8-3: Compromised data – Spotify credentials disclosed on the dark web. (Source: Recorded Future)

A high percentage of hacking-related breaches leverage stolen or weak passwords. Cybercriminals regularly upload massive caches of usernames and passwords to paste sites and the dark web, or make them available for sale on underground marketplaces. These data dumps can include corporate email addresses and passwords, as well as login details for other sites.

Monitoring external sources for this type of intelligence will dramatically increase your visibility, not just into leaked credentials, but also into potential breaches of corporate data and proprietary code.

Use case: Typosquatting and fraudulent domains

Typosquatting involves manipulating the characters in a company's domain name into nearly identical domains; for instance, example.com might become exanple.com. Attackers can register thousands of domains differing from target organizations' URLs by a single character for reasons ranging from suspicious to fully malicious. Rogue websites using these modified domain names are built to look like legitimate websites. The rogue domains and websites can be used in spearphishing campaigns against company employees or customers, watering-hole attacks, and drive-by download attacks.

Being alerted to newly registered phishing and typosquatting domains in real time narrows the window available for cybercriminals to impersonate your brand to defraud unsuspecting users. Once this malicious infrastructure is identified, you can employ a takedown service to nullify the threat.

ON THE WEB

We've already seen that criminal forums and marketplaces are well known for facilitating all types of clandestine transactions. But these channels are not the exclusive domain of criminal outsiders. A report from Recorded Future describes how corporate insiders advertise their access to criminal actors, as well as how employees and contractors are recruited into the criminal underground. Insiders are a useful cog in the machinery of fraud, from retail cash-out services, to carding operations, to theft facilitation by bank employees. Read the report "Insider Threats to Financial Services: Uncovering Evidence With External Intelligence."

Chapter 9

Threat Intelligence for Reducing Third-Party Risk

- Explore the impact of increasing third-party risk
- Understand why static assessment of third-party risk falls short
- See why using real-time, automated threat intelligence is the best way to mitigate third-party risk

"A chain is no stronger than its weakest link."

— Proverb

Third-Party Risk Looms Large

Because today's supply chains are so tightly integrated, we have to consider the security of our partners, vendors, and other third parties when assessing the risk profile of our own organization.

According to research firm ESG, most IT professionals believe that cyber risk management has become more difficult over the last two years. Many directly attribute this challenge to the additional effort required to manage third-party risk. Recent studies from the Ponemon Institute show that 59 percent of organizations have had a breach that originated from a third party, and only 29 percent believe their partners would notify them of a compromise. These and related statistics are shown in Figure 9-1.

59%
of organizations have
experienced a data
breach originated from
a third party

 29%
of organizations state that
a third party would notify
them of a data breach

 46%
of organizations always
audit the security risk
of third parties

What Recorded Future Knows About The World's Top Companies:

65%
have **exposed**
credentials

11%
are being **discussed**
on the **dark web**

Figure 9-1: Most organizations are exposed to significant risks through their relationships with third parties. Sources: Ponemon Institute and Recorded Future

The writing is on the wall: third-party attacks will get worse, they will further complicate cyber risk management, and your partners probably won't help you address the most critical problems.

Many traditional assessments of third-party risk rely on static outputs, like financial audits, monthly reports about new vulnerabilities discovered in systems an organization uses, and occasional reports on the status of security control compliance. These quickly go out of date and don't provide all the information you need to make informed decisions about how to manage risks.

In contrast, real-time threat intelligence enables you to accurately assess risk posed by third parties and keep assessments current as conditions change and new threats emerge.

Traditional Risk Assessments Fall Short

Many of the most common third-party risk management practices employed today lag behind security requirements. Static assessments of risk, like financial audits and security certificate verifications, are still important, but they often lack context and timeliness.

Organizations following traditional approaches to managing third-party risk often use these three steps:

1. They attempt to understand the organization's business relationship with a third party and how it exposes the organization to threats.

2. Based on that understanding, they identify frameworks to evaluate the third party's financial health, corporate controls, and IT security and hygiene, as well as how these relate to their organization's own approach to security.

3. Using those frameworks, the organization assesses the third party, determining whether it is compliant with security standards like SOC 2 or FISMA. Sometimes the company conducts a financial audit of the supplier or partner.

While these steps are essential for evaluating third-party risk, they don't tell the whole story. The output is static and cannot reflect quickly changing conditions and emerging threats. Often the analysis is too simplistic to produce actionable recommendations. Sometimes the final report is opaque, making it impossible to dig deeper into the methodology behind the analysis. That leaves decision-makers unsure about whether crucial bits of information might have been overlooked.

When assessing third-party risk, do not rely entirely on self-reporting questionnaires or a vendor's inwardly focused view of their security defenses. Round these out with an external, unbiased perspective on the vendor's threat landscape.

A Thought Experiment

Imagine that you went through the traditional steps of a static risk assessment, as outlined above. You concluded that one vendor in your supply chain is safe to work with.

Now this supplier experiences a data breach that may (or may not) have exposed your internal data. Can you accurately determine what, if any, proactive security measures you need to take and how quickly you should act?

Three Things to Look for in Threat Intelligence

To accurately evaluate third-party risk in real time, you need a solution that offers immediate context on the current threat landscape. Threat intelligence is one way to obtain that context and determine what shortcomings in the defenses of your supply chain partners represent significant risks to your organization. That added context includes not only current risks, but a historical view that can provide even more context to help detect, prevent, and resolve risks.

To help you evaluate third-party risk, a threat intelligence solution should offer:

1. Automation and machine learning to quickly and comprehensively sort massive amounts of data

2. Real-time alerts on threats and changes to risks

3. Transparency into the threat environments of your third-party partners

Automation and machine learning

To manage risk for your organization, you need access to massive amounts of threat data from the open web, the dark web, technical and news sources, and discussion forums. The same applies to assessing the risks of third parties.

But given the scale of cybersecurity-related content from these sources, totaling billions of facts, you need a threat intelligence solution that uses automation and artificial intelligence to collect and analyze these details. Your threat intelligence solution should be able to:

- ☑ Analyze, classify, and index data points using natural language processing capabilities and multiple machine learning models.

- ☑ Generate an objective, data-driven risk score using a straightforward mathematical formula

Real-time updates to risk scores

Static assessments quickly become outdated. Weekly or monthly intelligence reports produced by human analysts provide essential overviews, but often arrive too late to enable effective action.

Risk scoring is much more effective when it updates in real time and draws on a large pool of data. These capabilities make risk scores much more reliable for making immediate assessments and reaching security decisions.

For example, a trading partner might generally be regarded as low risk according to standard intelligence reporting. However, let's say the partner suffers a data breach that may (or may not) affect your organization. If you rely solely on static risk assessments, you likely won't know the breach happened in the first place, or not until it's too late. Or you may have to wait until it's too late to acquire the intelligence needed to accurately evaluate the risk. What was the cause of the breach? Was it an exploited vulnerability in the systems used by the partner? A social engineering attack? Static assessments will not provide the evidence needed to justify asking that third party to put additional security controls in place.

 ON THE WEB

Thomas H. Davenport is the President's Distinguished Professor of Information Technology and Management at Babson College, a Fellow of the MIT Center for Digital Business, an independent senior advisor to Deloitte Analytics, and the author of 15 books. He has written a report on the use of threat intelligence to generate risk scores that: (a) help executives and boards understand the high-level risk situations of partner companies; and (b) provide guidance to cyber intelligence teams on prioritizing investigations of third parties and their risks. The report, "Rating Companies on Third-Party Cyber Risk," is available at: https://go.recordedfuture.com/cyber-risk-scores.

Transparent risk assessments

What's the point of a risk assessment if you can't get anyone to act?

The problem of information without context leaves us like Cassandra in Greek mythology. In a bid for her love, the god Apollo gave her the gift of prophecy, but still she scorned his romantic advances. In his anger, he let her keep her foresight but cursed her so that nobody would ever believe her warnings about the future.

Many risk assessments today suffer the same fate as Cassandra's prophecies. When they rely on vague scoring methods or opaque sourcing, they can be hard to accept, even if they're accurate. Too often, organizations fail to act on intelligence because leaders don't understand it or don't know the source.

To help security professionals see for themselves why something like an alert on a particular IP address might represent a real risk, a threat intelligence solution should show the risk rules that are triggered by the alert and be transparent about its sources. The extra detail can also eliminate the suspicion that information might have been overlooked. This context allows for faster due diligence and reference checking, including when evaluating static assessments.

Figure 9-2: Threat intelligence provides context and helps identify shortcomings in the defenses of supply chain partners

Responding to High Third-Party Risk Scores

What do you do when faced with high risk scores for a third party? Not every data breach justifies terminating business with that partner. Just about every organization contends with cyberattacks and unexpected downtime, and partners are no exception. The more important issue is how they (and you) deal with incidents and take steps to reduce future risks.

A change in risk scores can present an opportunity to talk with your business partners about how they're approaching security. On your end, you can look more closely at whether the risk rules that were triggered will impact your organization's network. For example, a public partner's risk score might increase because typosquatting websites closely resembling legitimate websites operated by the partner were discovered. You can blacklist those sites in your own network to thwart phishing campaigns, and also investigate what steps that partner plans to take to protect its brand identity.

For smart security decisions, not knee-jerk reactions, you need up-to-the-minute context and evidence provided by threat intelligence.

Case Study: Insurance Company Gains Real-Time View of Third-Party Risk

For years, a Fortune 100 insurance company struggled to maintain a clear and current view of the risk profiles of its partners. The solution this organization relied on used data that was often outdated and rarely refreshed. The company couldn't see how a partner's risk score was trending over time and lacked visibility into specific events that were impacting the score.

This organization adopted a threat intelligence solution from Recorded Future that helps its security team better understand, analyze, and rapidly address third-party risks, including:

- Corporate emails, credentials, and company mentions found on the dark web

- Negative social media chatter

- Domain abuse (often indicative of phishing attacks)

- Use of vulnerable technologies

- IT infrastructure misuse or abuse

"[Recorded Future provides] valuable insights into the risk postures of the critical suppliers we do business with — from real-time risk scores and alerts to custom rules we've set — and allows us to drill deeper when needed," says the leader of the firm's third-party information risk management team. By prioritizing threat intelligence, the Recorded Future solution helps the team quickly:

- Rule out low-risk alerts and false positives

- Focus on the most significant threats

- Take immediate action to resolve them

This solution has helped the company reduce time spent on due diligence and reference checking by 50 percent, and replace a static, point-in-time approach with continuous monitoring.

You can find the full case study here: https://go.recordedfuture.com/hubfs/insurance-case-study.pdf

Chapter 10

Threat Intelligence for Digital Risk Protection

In this chapter

- Review the many forms of digital risk
- Learn how threat intelligence identifies many types of digital risk so they can be remediated

"Every contact leaves a trace."

— Locard's exchange principle of forensic science

Most of the chapters in this book describe how threat intelligence strengthens the work of specific teams in a cybersecurity organization. This chapter looks at how threat intelligence can help detect and remediate digital risks. This scenario spans the org chart, but still needs to be approached in a systematic, methodical way.

Digital risks come in many forms, as we discuss below. But the common denominator is the fact that most cyberattacks leave traces on the web. By finding those traces, threat intelligence gathering processes can pinpoint and remediate the most serious digital risks.

Being Online Is Being at Risk

These days, any business or individual wishing to make an impact must have a strong online presence. Aspiring artists, shrewd politicians, huge corporations, and start-ups alike strive to increase revenue, streamline business processes, and raise visibility through outward-facing websites, engagement with social media, and many other online activities.

A meaningful online presence requires you to think deeply about how to protect yourself from digital risk. Online engagement with your audience brings unwanted attention from threat actors of all sorts: financially motivated cybercriminals, competitors trying to obtain your secrets, and hacktivists who want to undermine your efforts. Some of them will succeed in capturing proprietary information.

You also have to worry about how threat actors can hijack your brand and counterfeit your web presence to serve their own ends — for example, by creating fraudulent domains to use in phishing attacks or by disseminating false information in your name.

Before we explore how threat intelligence can help thwart these threat actors, let's review some types of digital risk and the traces they leave on the web.

Types of Digital Risk

Digital risk falls into several categories. The most important are cyberattacks leading to the theft and disclosure of data, risks created by issues in the supply chain, risk related to actions by employees, and brand impersonation.

These risks are summarized in Figure 10-1.

	Attacks leading to unauthorized data disclosure	Cyberattacks can exploit vulnerabilities, misconfigurations, and inadequate security controls in IT and operational infrastructures. The latter type of infrastructure includes SCADA, DCS, and PLC systems that often lack basic defenses and are difficult or impossible to keep patched. Some cyberattacks leverage unsecure software coding practices. Social engineering attacks mislead employees into surrendering proprietary information or credentials that can be used to access internal systems.
	Supply Chain Issues	Business partners, suppliers, and other third parties that interact directly with your organization, but are not following the same security practices, can open the door to increased risk. Third-party risk is discussed at length in Chapter 9.
	Employee Risk	Even the most robust cybersecurity program can be subverted through social engineering efforts, compromise or manipulation of identity and access management systems, and insider attacks by disgruntled employees.
	Brand Impersonation	Sometimes attackers don't need to attack your systems directly; they are happy to use your brand to steal from your customers. Techniques include "typosquatting" (deploying websites that look like yours with a URL that is off by one character), creating social media accounts in your name, and offering mobile apps that claim to be yours but are under their control. Sometimes these impersonations of your web presence are elements of phishing attacks, and sometimes they are used by themselves to ensnare customers who mistype your URL or search for one of your social media accounts or apps. Either way, they can inflame distrust in your customer base and lead to significant loss of revenue.

Figure 10-1: Major categories of digital risk

Uncovering Evidence of Breaches on the Web

Threat intelligence solutions can pinpoint digital risks by monitoring the web, including private forums on the dark web, to uncover evidence of data breaches within your organization and partner ecosystem. Evidence can include:

- ☑ Your customers' names and data

- ☑ Financial account data and Social Security numbers

- ☑ Leaked or stolen credentials from your employees

- ☑ Paste and bin sites containing your proprietary software code

- ☑ Forums mentioning your company and announcing intentions to attack it

- ☑ Forums selling tools and discussing techniques to attack enterprises like yours

Timely discovery of these indicators can help you:

- ☑ Secure the sources of the data

- ☑ Find and fix vulnerabilities and misconfigurations in your infrastructure

- ☑ Mitigate future risks by improving security controls

- ☑ Identify ways to improve employee training and coding practices

- ☑ Enable your SOC and incident response teams to recognize attacks faster

TIP Often you can narrow down the source of a leak by looking at exactly what information and artifacts are found on the web, where they are found, and what else is found in the same place. For example, if you find product designs or software code on a dark web site and recognize that they were shared with only a few suppliers, you would know to investigate the security controls of those suppliers as part of your third-party risk management program. If your company's name was mentioned on a hacker's forum whose members are known to attack certain applications, you could increase protection of the targeted applications by patching the systems they run on, monitoring them more closely, and adding security controls.

Uncovering Evidence of Brand Impersonation and Abuse

Brand protection is a slightly different game than data protection. The primary goal is not to strengthen your infrastructure and security controls, but rather to "take down" (remove from the web) the impersonations as quickly as possible.

Threat data gathered from the web can reveal:

- ☑ Typosquatting domains

- ☑ Domain registrations that include your company or product name or variations

- ☑ Hashtags that include your company or product name or variations of them

☑ Social media accounts purporting to belong to you or one of your employees

☑ Unauthorized mobile apps using your branding

☑ Forums mentioning plans to impersonate your brand

Case Study: Defeating Typosquatting at a Large HR Solutions Provider

A large human resources, health, and wealth benefits solutions provider helps other organizations manage their human resources. This company handles a lot of personally identifiable information (PII), including sensitive health and financial data. To protect that data, they have an extensive security operations center, featuring 24/7/365 monitoring, incident response, investigation and forensics, and more.

Their vice president of security operations says that at one time it took a team of around 100 people to manage these functions. With Recorded Future, it takes 10. "Obtaining a list of all the mentions of our company across the Internet by the end of the day was totally infeasible, even if I had 10 or 20 people working on it," the VP says. "Sure, we could spend a lot of money to get people burner accounts and access to these private spaces, but what a waste! Anything beyond two people makes no sense compared to just using Recorded Future. The cost is less than two headcount, versus the 10 or 20 I would need to try to do something similar."

For example, one morning an alert went off about a potential typosquatting domain. This alert was triggered by a monitoring rule the team had set up in Recorded Future to check for fraudulent domains that resemble ones owned by the organization. Registering these domains is often the first step in a phishing attack.

As soon as the team got the alert, they investigated and found phishing attempts targeting both their organization and some of their clients. They immediately sent out a flash report to their whole organization and all their clients and partners. The report provided actionable recommendations on how to counter the attack: block the domain at your proxy and use these event logs to scan for the threat with your SIEM. Many of their partners reported hits from the site, but they were able to block access before any damage was done.

Thanks to real-time threat intelligence, the company was able to mitigate the threat in hours, rather than in weeks (or never).

Critical Qualities for Threat Intelligence Solutions

Of course, mitigating digital risk is not simply a matter of finding some isolated piece of stolen data or one typosquatting domain. Somebody, or something, has to do the broader work of collecting masses of data, sifting through thousands of data points, analyzing relationships among the data points, deciding priorities, and ultimately taking action.

The best approach is to use a threat intelligence solution that can:

☑ **Collect and scan data from the widest range of sources:** Automation at the data-collection stage saves analysts precious time. The best solutions gather data not only from open web sources, but also from the dark web and technical sources.

☑ **Map, monitor, and score digital risk:** Through automation, advanced data science, and analytic techniques like machine learning and natural language processing, threat intelligence solutions should help analysts link business attributes with related digital assets; detect, score, and prioritize digital risk events; and coordinate risk remediation activities.

☑ **Coordinate remediation:** Robust threat intelligence solutions generate alerts and reports that provide information on how to remediate problems. They also integrate with tools that can perform remediation immediately, and offer a service to take down typosquatting sites, misleading social media accounts, and other forms of brand impersonation.

Section 3: Your Threat Intelligence Program

Chapter 11

Analytical Frameworks for Threat Intelligence

- Learn about the advantages of using threat intelligence frameworks
- Understand the strengths and weaknesses of the three best-known frameworks
- See how the three frameworks can complement each other

"Structure is required for creativity."

— Twyla Tharp

Threat intelligence frameworks provide structures for thinking about attacks and adversaries. They promote a broad understanding of how attackers think, the methods they use, and where in an attack lifecycle specific events occur. This knowledge allows defenders to take decisive action faster and stop attackers sooner.

Frameworks also help focus attention on details that require further investigation to ensure that threats have been fully removed, and that measures are put in place to prevent future intrusions of the same kind.

Finally, frameworks are useful for sharing information within and across organizations. They provide a common grammar and syntax for explaining the details of attacks and how those details relate to each other. A shared framework makes it easier to ingest threat intelligence from sources such as threat intelligence vendors, open source forums, and information sharing and analysis centers (ISACs).

TIP The frameworks outlined below are not competitive, but rather complementary. You can utilize one, two, or all three of them.

The Lockheed Martin Cyber Kill Chain®

The Cyber Kill Chain®, first developed by Lockheed Martin in 2011, is the best known of the cyber threat intelligence frameworks. The Cyber Kill Chain is based on the military concept of the kill chain, which breaks the structure of an attack into stages. By breaking an attack up in this manner, defenders can pinpoint which stage it is in and deploy appropriate countermeasures.

The Cyber Kill Chain describes seven stages of an attack:

1. Reconnaissance
2. Weaponization
3. Delivery
4. Exploitation
5. Installation
6. Command and Control
7. Actions and Objectives (sometimes referred to as exfiltration)

These stages are often laid out in a diagram similar to Figure 11-1.

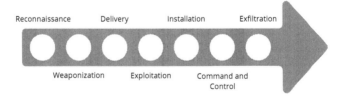

Figure 11-1: Diagram of the Lockheed Martin Cyber Kill Chain.

Security teams can develop standard responses for each stage.

For example, if you manage to stop an attack at the exploitation stage, you can have high confidence that nothing has been installed on the targeted systems and full incident response activity may not be needed.

The Cyber Kill Chain also allows organizations to build a defense-in-depth model that targets specific parts of the kill chain. For example, you might acquire third-party threat intelligence specifically to monitor:

☑ References to your enterprise on the web that would indicate reconnaissance activities

☑ Information about weaponization against newly reported vulnerabilities in applications on your network

Limitations of the Cyber Kill Chain

The Cyber Kill Chain is a good way to start thinking about how to defend against attacks, but it has some limitations. One of the big criticisms of this model is that it doesn't take into account the way many modern attacks work. For example, many phishing attacks skip the exploitation phase entirely, and instead rely on the victim to open a Microsoft Office document with an embedded macro or to double-click on an attached script.

But even with these limitations, the Cyber Kill Chain creates a good baseline to discuss attacks and where they can be stopped. It also makes it easier to share information about attacks within and outside of the organization using standard, well-defined attack points.

 You can find out more about the Cyber Kill Chain by reading the seminal white paper and visiting the Cyber Kill Chain website.

The Diamond Model

The Diamond Model was created in 2013 by researchers at the now-defunct Center for Cyber Intelligence Analysis and Threat Research (CCIATR). It is used to track attack groups over time rather than the progress of individual attacks.

In its simplest form, the Diamond Model looks similar to Figure 11-2. It is used to classify the different elements of an attack. The diamond for an attacker or attack group is not static, but rather evolves as the attacker changes infrastructure and targets and modifies TTPs.

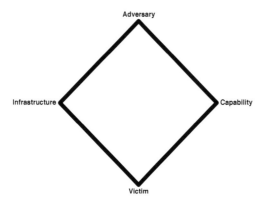

Figure 11-2: A simple Diamond Model design.

The Diamond Model helps defenders track an attacker, the victims, the attacker's capabilities, and the infrastructure the attacker uses. Each of the points on the diamond is a pivot point that defenders can use during an investigation to connect one aspect of an attack with the others.

Pivoting

Let's say you uncover command and control traffic to a suspicious IP address. The Diamond Model would help you "pivot" from this initial indicator to find information about the attacker associated with that IP address, then research the known capabilities of that attacker. Knowing those capabilities will enable you to respond more quickly and effectively to the incident. Or imagine that your threat intelligence solution uses the Diamond Model. If the board of directors asks who is launching similar attacks against other organizations in your industry (attribution), you may be able to quickly find a list of victims, the probable attacker, and a description of that attacker's TTPs. These will help you decide what defenses need to be put in place.

Flexibility

One of the big advantages of the Diamond Model is its flexibility and extensibility. You can add different aspects of an attack under the appropriate point on the diamond to create complex profiles of different attack groups. Other features of an attack that can be tracked include:

1. Phase

2. Result

3. Direction

4. Methodology

5. Resources

Challenges with the Diamond Model

The downside is that Diamond Models require a lot of care and feeding. Some aspects of the model, especially infrastructure, change rapidly. If you don't update the diamond of an attacker constantly, you run the risk of working with outdated information.

TIP Time stamp every update of a diamond so everybody has visibility into the age of the information.

TIP If you don't have the time and resources to manage this type of model yourself, you may be able to get updated information from a third-party threat intelligence provider.

Even with these challenges, though, the Diamond Model can make the jobs of many security people easier by helping get everyone fast answers about threats.

ON THE WEB To learn more about the Diamond Model, read the Recorded Future blog post "Applying Threat Intelligence to the Diamond Model of Intrusion Analysis", or download the original white paper "The Diamond Model of Intrusion Analysis."

The MITRE ATT&CK™ Framework

MITRE is a unique organization in the United States: a corporation responsible for managing federal funding for research projects across multiple federal agencies. It has had a huge impact on the security industry, including the development and maintenance of the Common Vulnerabilities and Exposures (CVE) and the Common Weakness Enumeration (CWE) databases.

MITRE has developed a number of other frameworks that are very important for threat intelligence, including:

☑ The Trusted Automated Exchange of Intelligence Information (TAXII™), a transport protocol that enables organizations to share threat intelligence over HTTPS and use common application programming interface (API) commands to extract that threat intelligence

☑ Structured Threat Information eXpression (STIX™), a standardized format for presenting threat intelligence information

☑ The Cyber Observable eXpression (CybOX™) framework, a method for tracking observables from cybersecurity incidents

Categories of attacker behavior

The MITRE Adversarial Tactics, Techniques, and Common Knowledge (ATT&CK™) framework was created as a means of tracking adversarial behavior over time. ATT&CK builds on the Cyber Kill Chain, but rather than describe a single attack, it focuses on the indicators and tactics associated with specific adversaries.

ATT&CK uses 11 different tactic categories to describe adversary behavior:

1. Initial Access

2. Execution

3. Persistence

4. Privilege Escalation

5. Defense Evasion

6. Credential Access

7. Discovery

8. Lateral Movement

9. Collection

10. Exfiltration

11. Command and Control

Each of these tactical categories includes individual techniques that can be used to describe the adversary's behavior. For example, under the Initial Access category, behaviors include Spearphishing Attachment, Spearphishing Link, Trusted Relationship, and Valid Accounts.

ON THE WEB You can see the MITRE Enterprise ATT&CK Framework at https://attack.mitre.org/wiki/Main_Page.

This classification of behaviors allows security teams to be very granular in describing and tracking adversarial behavior and makes it easy to share information between teams.

ATT&CK™ is useful across a wide range of security functions, from threat intelligence analysts to SOC operators and incident response teams. Tracking adversary behavior in a structured and repeatable way allows teams to:

☑ Prioritize incident response

☑ Tie indicators to attackers

☑ Identify holes in an organization's security posture

TIP Threat intelligence frameworks help codify the way your security teams look at threats, indicators, vulnerabilities, and actors. If you are not prepared to build out your own framework for analysis, consider partnering with security companies that have solutions built around these frameworks. That approach enables you to enjoy the benefits of the framework quickly and makes your security activities much more effective.

Chapter 12

Your Threat Intelligence Journey

- Review ways to clarify your threat intelligence needs and goals
- Examine key success factors that contribute to effective programs
- Learn how to start simple and scale up

"Whatever you do, or dream you can, begin it. Boldness has genius and power and magic in it."

— Johann Wolfgang von Goethe

In this chapter of our book, we suggest some do's and don'ts for starting on your threat intelligence journey and steering toward a comprehensive program.

Don't Start With Threat Feeds

In the first chapter we discussed several common misconceptions about threat intelligence, including that it is mostly about threat data feeds. In fact, many organizations begin their threat intelligence programs by signing up for threat data feeds and connecting them with a SIEM solution.

This may seem like a good way to start because many threat data feeds are open source (i.e., free), and the technical indicators they deliver appear useful and easy to interpret. Since all malware is bad, and every suspicious URL could be used by an attacker, the more clues you have about them the better, right?

Well, in reality, the vast majority of malware samples and suspicious URLs are not related to current threats to your enterprise. That's why feeding large volumes of unfiltered threat data to your SIEM will almost certainly create the kind of alert fatigue we examined in Chapter 4.

 ON THE WEB
To learn more about the range of threat intelligence sources, take a look at the Recorded Future blog post "Beyond Feeds: A Deep Dive Into Threat Intelligence Sources."

Clarify Your Threat Intelligence Needs and Goals

Because threat intelligence provides value to so many teams in cybersecurity, it is important to develop priorities that reflect the overall needs and goals of the enterprise.

Answer these questions

Rather than assuming that any one team, data source, or threat intelligence technology should have priority, you should develop a clear set of goals by determining the needs of each security group in your organization and the advantages that threat intelligence can bring to them.

Begin by considering these questions:

- ☑ What are your greatest risks?
- ☑ What are the ways that threat intelligence can help address each of those risks?
- ☑ What is the potential impact of addressing each risk?
- ☑ What gaps need to be filled by information, technology, or human resources to make threat intelligence effective in those areas?

Answering these questions will help you clarify where threat intelligence can deliver the biggest gains in the shortest time. It will also guide your investigation of which threat intelligence sources, tools, and vendors can best support you and what staff you need to strengthen your program.

The Recorded Future white paper "Best Practices for Applying Threat Intelligence" elaborates on why it is better to start out not by investigating technologies or vendors, but by looking first at the types of threat intelligence that are available and how they can make different areas of cybersecurity more effective.

Identify teams that can benefit most from threat intelligence

Teams across your security organization can benefit from intelligence that drives informed decision making and offers unique perspectives. Intelligence that is comprehensive, relevant, and easy to consume has the potential to revolutionize how different roles in your organization operate day to day. Figure 12-1 shows examples of how teams inside organizations can use threat intelligence.

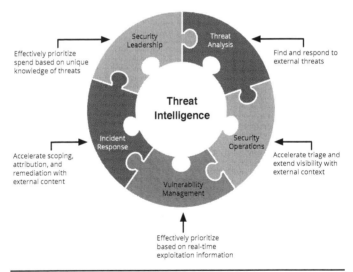

Figure 12-1: How security teams use threat intelligence.

When determining how to move your threat intelligence strategy forward, it's important to identify all the potential users in your organization and align the intelligence to their unique use cases.

DON'T FORGET

Drill down into the types of threat intelligence each group can use and exactly how they will benefit in terms of faster responses, lower costs, better use of staff, better investment decisions, etc. Often the needs and benefits are not obvious. Documenting these details will help you set priorities, justify investments, and find surprising new uses for threat intelligence.

ON THE WEB

Learn how threat intelligence can compensate for the talent gap that many companies face by reading the Recorded Future blog post "Threat Analyst Insights: Threat Intelligence as a Leveler."

Key Success Factors

We have observed several factors that frequently contribute to effective threat intelligence programs.

Generating quick wins with monitoring

Monitoring threat information can provide quick benefits with relatively modest investments. The key is to look for a few types of data that are particularly meaningful for your business and information security strategy and will help you anticipate emerging threats or provide early warning of actual attacks. Your activities might include things like:

- ☑ Checking for new vulnerabilities that affect your most important software packages, servers, and endpoints
- ☑ Tracking threat trends that pose potential risks to your business operations
- ☑ Watching for any leaked corporate credentials, data, or code appearing on public or dark web sites

There are probably a few data types that are vitally important to your business and that you can monitor without investing in new infrastructure or staff. Monitoring them can generate quick wins, demonstrate the advantages of threat intelligence, and build enthusiasm for the program.

Automating as much as possible

Effective threat intelligence programs typically focus on automation from the beginning. They start by automating fundamental tasks like data aggregation, comparison, labeling, and contextualization. When these tasks are performed by machines, humans are freed up to work on making effective, informed decisions.

As your threat intelligence program becomes more sophisticated, you may find even more opportunities for automation. You will be able to automate information sharing among a larger group of security solutions and automate more workflows that provide intelligence to incident analysis and response and fraud prevention teams. You will be able to offload more of the "thinking" to your threat intelligence solutions, for example, by having the software automatically correlate threat data and produce risk scores.

When you evaluate threat intelligence solutions, examine the level to which they employ automation. Is automation confined to aggregating and cross-referencing data, or does the solution add context that equips your teams to make risk-based decisions with confidence? Keep in mind that in threat intelligence, more raw data only adds value if it's properly analyzed, structured, and delivered to you in an easy-to-consume format.

Integrating threat intelligence with processes and infrastructure

Integrating threat intelligence tools with existing systems is an effective way to make the intelligence accessible and usable without overwhelming teams with new technologies.

Part of integration is giving threat intelligence tools visibility into the security events and activities captured by your other security and network tools. Combining and correlating internal and external data points can produce genuine intelligence that is both relevant to your business and placed in the context of the wider threat landscape.

The other critical aspect of integration is delivering the most important, specific, relevant, and contextualized intelligence to the right group at the right time.

Threat intelligence solutions can be integrated with SIEMs and other security tools either through APIs or interfaces developed in partnership with the security tool vendors.

TIP

When you evaluate threat intelligence solutions, it's important to understand which ones can integrate with your existing software and support your security teams' use cases.

Getting expert help to nurture internal experts

The value you get from threat intelligence is directly related to your ability to make it relevant to your organization and apply it to existing and new security processes.

You can reach these goals faster if you work with a vendor or consultant that provides both technical capabilities and expertise to empower your organization to get the most from threat intelligence. As time goes on, working with such a partner will enable members of your team to become threat intelligence experts in their own right, so that your capabilities in the field can grow organically.

DON'T FORGET

Look for partners with a wide and deep bench of threat intelligence experts. These specialists should be equipped to understand your needs and ready to help you get the most from your investment. You should be able to call on their expertise as needed and to work with them to identify new advantages from leveraging threat intelligence in your organization. Your chosen partners should not only help you succeed today, but also support your security teams as you move forward.

ON THE WEB

You can get more information on selecting the right threat intelligence solution by downloading "The Buyer's Guide to Cyber Threat Intelligence," from Recorded Future. It includes a handy RFP template to use in evaluating the capabilities of different vendors.

Start Simple and Scale Up

We hope this book has shown you that threat intelligence is not some kind of monolith that needs to be dropped onto the security organization all at one time. Instead, you have options to draw on a wide range of data sources and then process, analyze, and disseminate threat intelligence to every major group in cybersecurity.

That means you can start simple with your current staff (instead of a dedicated threat intelligence group), a few data sources, and integration with existing security tools like SIEM and vulnerability management systems. You can then scale up to dedicated staffing, more data sources, more tools, more integration, and more automated workflows, as shown in Figure 12-2.

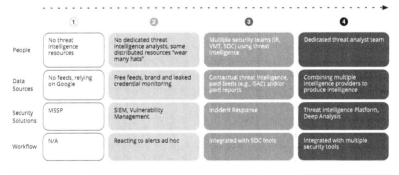

Figure 12-2: Four stages of maturity for threat intelligence programs, from no internal resources, to limited sources and tools, to a fully staffed, highly automated threat intelligence program.

Start the journey by researching the needs of each group in your cybersecurity organization and seeing how threat intelligence can help them achieve their objectives.

Then, over time, you can build toward a comprehensive threat intelligence program that:

- ☑ Scours the widest possible range of technical, open, and dark web sources
- ☑ Uses automation to deliver easily consumable intelligence
- ☑ Provides fully contextualized alerts in real time with limited false positives
- ☑ Integrates with and enhances existing security technologies and processes
- ☑ Consistently improves the efficiency and efficacy of your entire security organization

Chapter 13

Developing the Core Threat Intelligence Team

- Understand the processes, people, and technology that make up a dedicated threat intelligence capability
- Learn how these teams use threat intelligence not just to judge risk, but also to drive business continuity
- Review ways to engage with threat intelligence communities

"Talent wins games, but teamwork and intelligence win championships."

— Michael Jordan

We have seen how threat intelligence benefits most of the teams in the information security organization. We now make a few suggestions about how to organize your core threat intelligence team itself.

Dedicated, but Not Necessarily Separate

As we discussed in the previous chapter, you can start your threat intelligence journey with people who continue to play other roles on different teams in the organization.

Two questions will arise:

1. Should there be a dedicated threat intelligence team?
2. Should it be independent, or can it live inside another cybersecurity group?

The answers are: yes, and it depends.

A dedicated team is best

As you develop a comprehensive threat intelligence program, you should build a team dedicated to collecting and analyzing threat data and turning it into intelligence. The sole focus of this team should be to provide relevant and actionable intelligence to key stakeholders, including senior executives and members of the board.

Dedication and a broad perspective are needed to ensure team members dedicate enough time to collecting, processing, analyzing, and disseminating intelligence that provides the greatest value to the enterprise as a whole, rather than yielding to the temptation to focus on the intelligence needs of one group or another.

Its location depends on your organization

Organizational independence, as shown in Figure 13-1, has its advantages, such as greater autonomy and prestige.

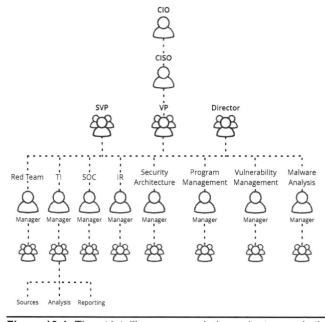

Figure 13-1: Threat intelligence as an independent group in the cybersecurity organizational structure.

However, these advantages can be completely offset by the jealousies and political issues caused by creating a team with a new high-level manager and its own budget that pulls budding threat intelligence analysts out of their existing groups.

A dedicated threat intelligence team does not necessarily need to be a separate function reporting directly to a VP or the CISO. It can belong to a group that already works with threat intelligence. In many cases this will be the incident response group. This savvy approach can avoid conflict with entrenched security teams.

Picking the People

If you take a gradual approach to building your core threat intelligence team, start with individuals who are already in the cybersecurity organization and are applying threat intelligence to their particular areas of security. They may not have the title "threat intelligence analyst" or see themselves that way at first, but they can form the backbone of your emerging threat intelligence capability.

Core Competencies

We have emphasized that the threat intelligence function exists to strengthen other teams in the cybersecurity organization so they can better protect a specific enterprise. It is therefore critical that the threat intelligence team include people who understand the core business, operational workflows, network infrastructure, risk profiles, and supply chain as well as the technical infrastructure and software applications of the entire enterprise.

As the threat intelligence team matures, you'll want to add members with skills for:

- ☑ Correlating external data with internal telemetry
- ☑ Providing threat situational awareness and recommendations for security controls

- ☑ Proactively hunting internal threats, including insider threats
- ☑ Educating employees and customers on cyber threats
- ☑ Engaging with the wider threat intelligence community
- ☑ Identifying and managing information sources

Collecting and Enriching Threat Data

We talked a little about sources of threat data in Chapter 2. Here we explore how a threat intelligence team can work with a range of sources to ensure accuracy and relevance.

The human edge

Threat intelligence vendors can provide some types of strategic intelligence, but you can also develop in-house capabilities to gather information about the topics and events most relevant to your enterprise.

For example, you could develop an internal web crawler that analyzes the web page code of the top 5,000 web destinations visited by your employees. This analysis might provide insights into the potential for drive-by download attacks. You could share the insights with the security architecture team to help them propose controls that defend against those attacks. This kind of threat intelligence generates concrete data, which is much more useful than anecdotes, conjecture, and generic statistics about attacks.

Additional sources

Proprietary sources that can strengthen your threat intelligence resources include:

- ☑ Vendor or ISAC feeds
- ☑ Whitelists
- ☑ Blacklists
- ☑ Threat intelligence team research

Combining sources

An automated threat intelligence solution enables the threat intelligence team to centralize, combine, and enrich data from multiple sources before the data is ingested by other security systems or viewed by human analysts on security operations teams.

Figure 13-2 shows the elements of such an automated threat solution. In this process, information from a threat intelligence vendor is filtered to find data that is important to the enterprise and specific cybersecurity teams. Then it is enriched by data from internal threat intelligence sources and output in formats appropriate for targets such as SIEMs and incident response systems. This automated translation of data into relevant insights is the very essence of threat intelligence.

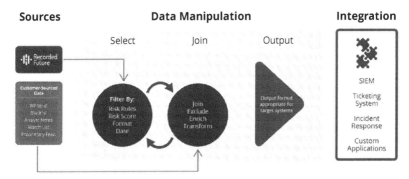

Figure 13-2: A threat intelligence platform can centralize, combine, and enrich data, then format it for multiple target systems. (Source: Recorded Future)

The role of intelligent machines

Advances in machine learning and natural language processing (NLP) can bring additional advantages to the threat intelligence team. With the right technology, references to threats from all sources can be rendered language-neutral, so it can be analyzed by humans and machines regardless of the original language used. We've reached the point where AI components have successfully learned the language of threats and can accurately identify "malicious" terms.

The combination of machine learning, NLP, and AI offers huge opportunities for organizations to leverage threat intelligence. Not only can these technologies remove language barriers, but they also can reduce analyst workloads by taking on many tasks related to data collection and correlation. When combined with the power to consider multiple data and information sources concurrently to produce genuine threat intelligence, these capabilities make it far easier to build a comprehensible map of the threat landscape.

ON THE WEB See how Recorded Future applies advanced AI in the white paper "4 Ways Machine Learning Is Powering Smarter Threat Intelligence."

ON THE WEB You can find out how financial services giant Fannie Mae streamlined the communication of finished intelligence by reading "How to Build a Cyber Threat Intelligence Team (and Why Technology Isn't Enough)" on the Recorded Future blog.

Engaging With Threat Intelligence Communities

Threat intelligence cannot flourish in a vacuum. External relationships are the lifeblood of successful threat intelligence teams. No matter how advanced your team might be, no single group can be as smart individually as the threat intelligence world as a whole.

Many threat intelligence communities allow individual enterprises to share relevant and timely attack data so they can protect themselves before they are victimized. Engaging with trusted communities such as ISACs is crucial for decreasing risk, not just for your individual enterprises, but also for the entire industry and the cybersecurity world at large. Participation requires time and resources, for example to communicate with peers via email and to attend security conferences, but relationship building must be a priority for threat intelligence to be successful.

Conclusion: Moving Toward a Security Intelligence Program

"Know your enemy and know yourself and you can fight a hundred battles without disaster."

— Sun Tzu

Key Takeaways From the Book

We began this guide by introducing the premise that intelligence helps everyone in cybersecurity, enabling teams to anticipate threats, respond to attacks faster, and make better decisions on how to reduce risk. In the 13 chapters contained in this book, we examined how intelligence can be applied to numerous facets of an organization's security strategy, enabling a shift toward a more proactive, comprehensive security approach.

This is security intelligence — an approach that amplifies the effectiveness of security teams and tools by exposing unknown threats, informing better decisions, and driving a common understanding to ultimately accelerate risk reduction across the organization. With the three pillars of threat intelligence, digital risk protection, and third-party risk reduction, all organizations can get real insight into the risks they face, and streamline how their teams work to make better use of valuable human resources.

As explained in the foreword to this book, a security intelligence approach is rooted in three principles:

> **1. Threat intelligence must provide the context to make informed decisions and take action.**

Threat intelligence needs to be timely, clear, and actionable. It has to come at the right time, in a form that is understandable. It should enrich your knowledge, not complicate the decision-making process. It should help put everybody in your organization on the same page.

2. People and machines work better together.

Machines can process and categorize raw data orders exponentially faster than humans. On the other hand, humans can perform intuitive, big-picture analysis much better than any artificial intelligence — as long as they're not overwhelmed with sorting through huge data sets and doing tedious research. When people and machines are paired, each works smarter, saving time and money, reducing human burnout, and improving security overall.

3. Threat intelligence is for everyone.

No matter what security role you serve, threat intelligence makes a difference. It's not a separate domain of security — it's context that helps you work smarter, whether you're staffing a SOC, managing vulnerabilities, or making high-level security decisions. But to make things easier, not harder, threat intelligence should integrate with the solutions and workflows on which you already rely, and should be easy to implement.

Whether you are just kicking off your security intelligence initiative or you are many years into your strategy, efficiently reducing risk is the ultimate goal.

Appendix

Threat Intelligence Goals: A Quick Reference Guide

Threat intelligence is not "one size fits all." The security applications of threat intelligence in your business depend on the nature of your organization and your existing information security strategies and capabilities.

This library of threat intelligence goals aligns with the security teams we have highlighted in this book. You can use these goals to help identify and prioritize threat intelligence activities.

Security Operations	
Data Exposure Incidents	Report data exposure incidents to affected stakeholders for remediation
High-Risk Malware Families	Research evolution and trends of malware families with high risk to my organization
Reputation Risk	Identify risks to my organization's reputation
Incident Response	
Data Exposure Incidents	Report data exposure incidents to affected parties and stakeholders for remediation
Vulnerability Management	
Exploit Kits	Identify information about exploit kits
High-Risk Vulnerabilites	Identify critical and high-risk vulnerabilities in tech stack
Undisclosed Vulnerabilities	Identify undisclosed zero-day and embargoed vulnerabilities
Risk Analysis	
Third-Party Security Competence	Assess third party's information security competence
Third Parties With Elevated Risk	Identify third parties that have elevated risk to my organization
Competitive Research	Research competitive market
Security Leadership	
Third Parties With Elevated Risk	Identify third parties that have elevated risk to my organization
Attack Planning	Identify attack planning that could target my organization

Industry Attack Trends	Identify campaigns targeting related industries
Infrastructure Risk	Increased risk score for my infrastructure
Phishing and Spam Campaign Trends	Identify trending campaigns that use spearphishing or phishing with malicious email attachments or links
Reputation Risk	Identify risks to my organization's reputation
Targeted Campaign Research	Identify IOCs associated with a specific operation or campaign to help track and mitigate cyberattacks
Targeted Threat Actor Research	Identify IOCs associated with threat actors to help track and mitigate cyberattacks
Fraud Prevention	
Stolen Asset Discovery	Discover stolen assets (e.g., gift cards, credit cards) posted online
Threat Intelligence Analysis	
Third Parties With Elevated Risk	Identify third parties that have elevated risk to my organization
Data Exposure Incidents	Report data exposure incidents to affected parties and stakeholders for remediation
Exploit Kits	Identify information about exploit kits
High-Risk Malware Families	Research evolution and trends of malware families with high risk to me
High-Risk Vulnerabilities	Identify critical and high-risk vulnerabilities in tech stack
Identify Attack Planning	Identify attack planning that could target my organization
Industry Attack Trends	Identify campaigns targeting related industries
Infrastructure Risk	Increased risk score for my infrastructure
Phishing and Spam Campaign Trends	Identify trending campaigns that use spearphishing or phishing with malicious email attachments or links
Reputation Risk	Identify risks to my organization's reputation
Targeted Campaign Research	Identify IOCs associated with a specific operation or campaign to help track and mitigate cyberattacks
Targeted Threat Actor Research	Identify IOCs associated with threat actors to help track and mitigate cyberattacks
Undisclosed Vulnerabilities	Identify undisclosed zero-day and embargoed vulnerabilities